Suicide by Democracy

an Obituary for America and the World

Michael Starks

Reality Press   Las Vegas

ISBN-13: 978-1987415544

PREFACE

"At what point is the approach of danger to be expected? I answer, if it ever reach us it must spring up amongst us; it cannot come from abroad. If destruction be our lot, we must ourselves be its author and finisher. As a nation of freemen we must live through all time or die by suicide." Abraham Lincoln (1838)

Among the millions of pages of print and web pages and incessant chat and chatter on TV and blogs and speeches, there is a notable absence of a short clear honest, accurate, sane, intelligent summary of the catastrophe that is destroying America and the world. This is partly due to a lack of understanding and partly to the suppression of free speech by the leftist/liberal/progressive/democratic/socialist/multicultural/diverse/social democratic/communist/third world supremacist coalition. I attempt to fill that gap here.

An integral part of modern democracy is The One Big Happy Family Delusion, i.e., that we are selected for cooperation with everyone, and that the euphonious ideals of Democracy, Diversity and Equality will lead us into utopia, if we just manage things correctly (the possibility of politics). The No Free Lunch Principle ought to warn us it cannot be true, and we see throughout history and all over the contemporary world, that without strict controls, selfishness and stupidity gain the upper hand and soon destroy any nation that embraces these delusions. In addition, the monkey mind steeply discounts the future, and so we cooperate in selling our descendant's heritage for temporary comforts, greatly exacerbating the problems.

I describe the great tragedy playing out in America and the world, which can be seen as a direct result of our evolved psychology, which, though eminently adaptive and eugenic on the plains of Africa ca. 6 million years ago, when we split from chimpanzees, to ca. 50,000 to 150,000 years ago, when many of our ancestors left Africa (i.e., in the EEA or Environment of Evolutionary Adaptation), is now maladaptive and dysgenic and the source of our Suicidal Utopian Delusions. So, like all discussions of behavior (philosophy, psychology, sociology, biology, anthropology, politics, law, literature, history, economics, soccer strategies, business meetings, etc.), this book is ultimately about evolutionary strategies, selfish genes and inclusive fitness (kin selection, i.e., natural selection).

One might take this to imply that a just, democratic and enduring society for any kind of entity on any planet in any universe is only a dream, and that no being or power could make it otherwise. It is not only 'the laws' of physics that are universal and inescapable, or perhaps we should say that inclusive fitness is a law of physics.

The great mystic Osho said that the separation of God and Heaven from Earth and Humankind was the most evil idea that ever entered the human mind. In recent times an even more evil notion arose, that humans are born with rights, rather than having to earn privileges. The idea of human rights, as now commonly promulgated, is an evil fantasy created by leftists to draw attention away from the merciless destruction of the earth by unrestrained 3rd world motherhood. Thus, every day the population increases by 200,000, who must be provided with resources to grow and space to live, and who soon produce another 200,000 etc. And one almost never hears it noted that what they receive must be taken from those already alive, and their descendants. Their lives diminish those already here in both major obvious and countless subtle ways. Every new baby destroys the earth from the moment of conception. In a horrifically overcrowded world with vanishing resources, there cannot be human rights without destroying the earth and our descendants futures. It could not be more obvious, but it is rarely mentioned in a clear and direct way, and one will never see the streets full of protesters against motherhood.

The most basic fact, almost never mentioned, is that there are not enough resources in America or the world to lift a significant percentage of the poor out of poverty and keep them there. The attempt to do this is bankrupting America and destroying the world. The earth's capacity to produce food decreases daily, as does our genetic quality. And now, as always, by far the greatest enemy of the poor is other poor and not the rich.

America and the world are in the process of collapse from excessive population growth, most of it for the last century, and now all of it, due to 3rd world people. Consumption of resources, and the addition of some 3 billion more ca. 2100, will collapse industrial civilization and bring about starvation, disease, violence and war on a staggering scale. The earth loses about 2% of its topsoil every year, so as it nears 2100, most of its food growing capacity will be gone. Billions will die and nuclear war is all but certain. In America, this is being hugely accelerated by massive immigration and immigrant reproduction, combined with abuses made possible by democracy. Depraved human nature inexorably turns the dream of democracy and diversity into a nightmare of crime and poverty. China will continue to overwhelm America and the world, as long as it maintains the dictatorship which limits selfishness.

The root cause of collapse is the inability of our innate psychology to adapt to the modern world, which leads people to treat unrelated persons as though they had common interests (which I suggest may be regarded as an unrecognized -- but the commonest and most serious-- psychological problem -- Inclusive Fitness Disorder). This, plus ignorance of basic biology and psychology, leads to the social engineering delusions of the partially educated who control democratic societies. Few understand that if you help one person you harm someone else—there is no free lunch and every single item anyone consumes destroys the earth beyond repair. Consequently, social policies everywhere are unsustainable and one by one all societies without stringent controls on selfishness will collapse into anarchy or dictatorship. Without dramatic and immediate changes, there is no hope for preventing the collapse of America, or any country that follows a democratic system.

Those interested in further applications of these ideas may consult my other books, particularly Suicidal Utopian Delusions in the 21st Century: Philosophy, Human Nature and the Collapse of Civilization, which are available free at various sites on the net as well as on Amazon as books and Kindles:

https://www.amazon.com/dp/B071P1RP1B
https://www.amazon.com/dp/B0711R5LGX
https://www.amazon.com/dp/B071HVC7YP

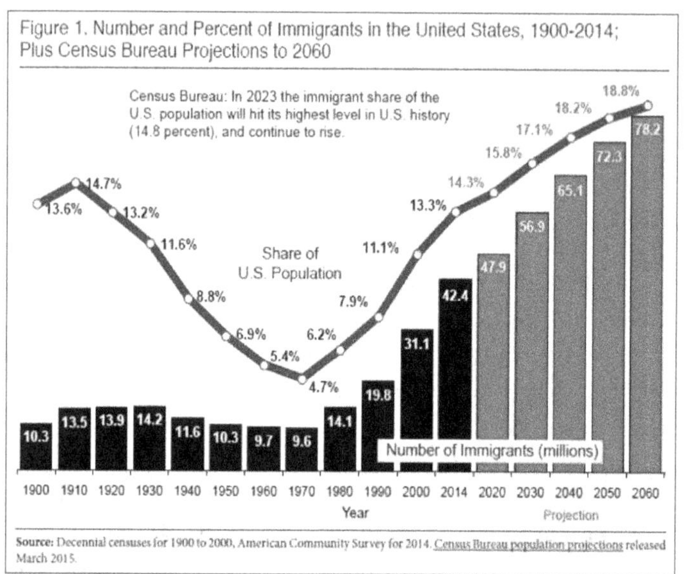

Figure 1. Number and Percent of Immigrants in the United States, 1900-2014; Plus Census Bureau Projections to 2060

Source: Decennial censuses for 1900 to 2000, American Community Survey for 2014. Census Bureau population projections released March 2015.

PERCENT OF AMERICANS WHO ARE FOREIGN BORN -- the result of the "no significant demographic impact" immigration act of 1965—non-Europeans (the Diverse) were a 16% share, are now (2016) 37% and will be about 60% by 2100, since they are now 100% of the population increase of about 2.4 million every year. Suicide by democracy.

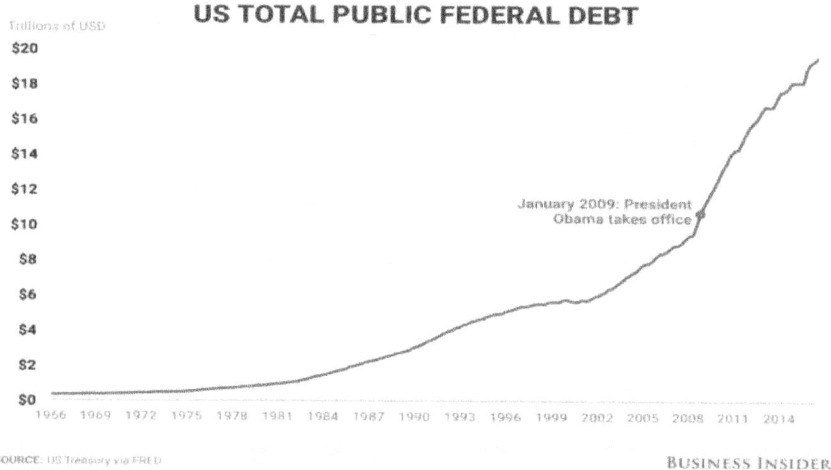

PART OF THE COST OF DIVERSITY and of aging, being the world's unpaid policeman, etc., (not counting future liabilities which are 5 to 10 times as much, barring major social changes).

Useful definitions for understanding American politics

DIVERSITY: 1. USA government program for handing over control to Mexico. 2. USA government program for providing free or heavily subsidized goods and services to those from other countries. 3. A means for turning America into a 3rd world Hellhole. 4. Multiculturalism, multiethnicism, multipartisanism, inclusivity, third world supremacy.

RACIST: 1. Person opposed to diversity in above sense. 2. Person of different ethnicity who disagrees with me on any issue. 3. Person of any ethnicity who disagrees with me on anything. Also, called 'bigot' 'hater' or 'nativist'.

WHITE SUPREMACIST: Anyone opposed to diversity in the above sense, i.e., anyone trying to prevent the collapse of America and of industrial civilization worldwide.

THIRD WORLD SUPREMACIST: Anyone in favor of diversity in above senses. Anyone working to destroy their descendant's future. AKA Democrats, Socialists, Democratic Socialists, Marxists, Leftists, Liberals, Progressives, Communists, Maternalists, Leftist Fascists, Multiculturalists, Inclusivists, Human Rightists.

HATE: 1. Any opposition to diversity in the above sense. 2. Expression of a desire to prevent the collapse of America and the world.

EURO: White or Caucasian or European: one whose ancestors left Africa over 50,000 years ago.

BLACK: African or Afro-American: one whose ancestors stayed in Africa or left in the last few hundred years (so there has not been time for evolution of any significant differences from Euros).

DIVERSE: Anyone who is not EURO (European, white, Caucasian).

HUMAN RIGHTS: An evil fantasy created by leftists to draw attention away from the merciless destruction of the earth by unrestrained 3rd world montherhood. Thus, temporary anomalies, such as democracy, equality, labor unions, women's rights, child rights, animal rights, etc. are due to high standards of living created by the rape of the planet and will disappear as civilization collapses.

I should first note that I have no investment in the outcome of any social or political movement. I am old, without kids or close relatives, and in the blink of an eye I will be gone (of course the most important thing to remember is that very soon we will all be gone and our descendants will face the horrific consequences of our stupidity and selfishness). I offer these comments in hope they will give perspective, since concise rational competent analyses of the perilous situation in America and the world are almost nonexistent. I have have close friends of various ethnicities, several times given my only assets to an impoverished third world person (no I did not inherit anything significant, did not have rich relatives, a trust fund or a cushy job), have had third world friends, colleagues, girlfriends, wives and business partners, and helped anyone in any way I could regardless of race, age, creed, sexual preferences or national origin and am still doing so. I have not voted in any kind of election, belonged to any religious, social or political group, listened to a political speech or read a book on politics in over 50 years, as I considered it pointless and demeaning. I find nearly all political dialog to be superficial, mistaken and useless. This is my first and last social/political commentary.

The millions of daily articles, speeches, tweets and newsbites rarely mention it, but what is happening in America and worldwide are not some transient and unconnected events, but the infinitely sad story of the inexorable collapse of industrial civilization due to overpopulation. Though this is the only important issue, it seldom comes up in the endless debates and daily social convulsions, and few things in this article are ever discussed in any clear and intelligent way, in large part because the Diverse (i.e., those not of European ancestry) have a strangle hold on American and most Western media which make it impossible. Politics in democratic countries is dedicated almost entirely to providing the opportunity for every special interest group to get an ever-bigger share of the rapidly diminishing resources. The problem is that nearly all people are short-sighted, selfish, poorly educated, lacking experience and stupid and this creates an insoluble problem when there are 10 billion (by century's end), or when they constitute a majority of any electorate in a democratic system. It's one thing to make mistakes when there are time and resources to correct them, but quite another when it's impossible. The USA is the worst case as it seems to have vast resources and a resilient economy, and what I and most people grew up regarding as the wonderful traditions of justice, democracy, and equality, but I now see that these are invitations to exploitation by every special interest group and that giving privileges to everyone born, without imposing duties, has fatal consequences. Also, a system that operates this way cannot compete with ones that do not- Asia is eating America's lunch (and that of all non-Asian countries), and nothing can stop it, but of course overpopulation dooms everyone (the minority who will survive after the great 22nd/23rd century die-off) to a hellish life. A world where everyone is free to replicate their genes and consume resources as they wish will soon have a hard landing. The fact is that democracy has become a license to steal- from the government—i.e., from the shrinking minority who pay significant taxes, from the earth, from everyone everywhere, and from one's own descendants, and that diversity (multiculturalism, multipartisanism, etc.) in an overcrowded world leads to insoluble conflict and collapse.

The history in America is clear enough. In what can now be seen as the first major disaster stemming from the lunatic Christian idea of innate human rights, the politicians of the Northern states decided it was inappropriate for the South to have slaves. Slavery was certainly an outmoded and evil idea and was disappearing worldwide, and it would have been eliminated with economic and political pressures after emancipation via the 13th amendment. But then as now the utopian delusions prevailed, and so they attacked the South, killing and crippling millions and creating poverty and dysgenic chaos (the death and debility of a large percentage of able bodied males) whose effects are still with us. The Africans replicated their genes at a higher rate, resulting in their coming to comprise an ever-increasing percentage of the country. Nobody realized it at the time and most still do not, but this was the beginning of the collapse of America and the defects in psychology which led the North to persecute the South were a continuation of the Christian fanaticisms which produced the murder and torture of millions during the middle ages, the Inquisition, the genocide of the new world Indians by the Europeans, the Crusades and the Jihads of the muslims for the last 1200 years. ISIS, Al-Queda, the Crusaders and the Army of the North have a great deal in common.

Without asking the voters, a few thousand statesmen and congressmen and President Lincoln made ex-slaves citizens and gave them the right to vote via the 14th and 15th amendments. Gradually there came to be vast ghettos composed of ex slaves, where crime and poverty flourished, and where drugs (imported mostly by Hispanics) generated a vast criminal empire, whose users committed hundreds of millions of crimes every year. Then came the Democrats led by the Kennedys, who, raised in privilege and disconnected from the real world, and having like nearly all politicians no clue about biology, psychology, human ecology or history, decided in 1965 that it was only democratic and just that the country should change the immigration laws to decrease influx of Europeans in favor of 3rd world people (the Diverse). They passed the law and in 1965 president Lyndon Johnson signed it (see cover photo). There were misgivings from some quarters that this would destroy America, but they were assured that there would be "no significant demographic impact"! The American public never (to this day in 2018) had a chance to express their views (i.e., to vote), unless you count the Trump election as that chance, and congress and various presidents changed our democracy into a "Socialist Democracy", i.e., into a semi-communist state enforced by fascism. The Chinese are delighted as they do not have to fight the USA for dominance, but only to wait for it to collapse.

A few decades ago, William Brennen, Chief Justice of the Supreme Court, suggested that a law passed a century before, to guarantee citizenship to former slaves (the first fatal legislative mistake, the second giving them the vote), should apply to anyone who happened to be born in America. Subsequently, other rulings of the court (not the people, who have never been asked) decided all those born in the USA, regardless of parental status (e.g., even if they were aliens from another solar system) had a right to US citizenship (anchor babies) and were permitted to make citizens of all their relatives – (the third and fourth fatal mistakes). Again, it never crossed the minds of congress or the courts that the constitution did not give any such rights, nor that the American public should be permitted to vote on this. In addition to the millions of 3rd world people here "legally" (i.e., with the permission of a few hundred in congress, but not the people) millions began entering illegally and all produced children at about 3 times the rate of existing Americans and generated ever increasing social problems. Most of the Diverse pay little or no taxes, and so they live partly or wholly on government handouts (i.e., taxes paid by the ever shrinking minority of Americans who pay any, as well as money borrowed from future generations to the tune of $2.5 billion a day, added to the $18 trillion in debt and the $90 trillion or more of unfunded future obligations—medicare, social security etc.), while the agricultural system, housing, streets and highways, sewers, water and electrical systems, parks, schools, hospitals, courts, public transportation, government, police, fire, emergency services and the huge defense spending needed to ensure the continued existence of the country, were created, staffed and largely paid for by Euros (i.e., those of European ancestry). The fact that the Diverse owe their well-being (relative to the Diverse still in the 3rd world) and their very existence (medicine, technology, agriculture, suppression of war and slavery) to Euros is never mentioned by anyone (see below).

Naturally, the Euros (and a minority of tax paying Diverse) are outraged to have to spend ever more of their working lives to support the legions of newly arrived Diverse, to be unsafe in their own homes and streets and to see their towns, schools, hospitals, parks etc. being taken over and destroyed. They try to protest, but the media are now controlled by the Diverse (with the help of deluded Euros who are dedicated to destroying their own descendants), and it is now almost impossible to state any opposition to the collapse of America without being attacked as "racist", "white supremacist" or "a hater", and often losing one's job for exercising free speech. Words referring to the Diverse are almost banned, unless it's to praise them and assist their genuine racism (i.e., living at the expense of and exploiting and abusing in every way possible the Euro's, and their Diverse tax paying neighbors), so one cannot mention blacks, immigrants, Hispanics, Muslims etc. in the same discussion with the words rapist, terrorist, thief, murderer, child molester, convict, criminal, welfare etc., without being accused of "hatred" or "racism" or "white supremacy". They are of course oblivious to their own racism and third world supremacy. Keep in mind there is not and almost certainly will never be any evidence of a significant genetic difference between Euros and Diverse in psychology, or IQ, and that their tendency to excessive reproduction and other shortcomings is wholly due to culture.

Gradually, every kind of special interest group has succeeded in eliminating any negative reference to them in any easily identifiable way, so there has almost vanished from public discourse not only words referring to the Diverse, but to the short, tall, fat, thin, mentally ill, handicapped, genetically defective, disadvantaged, abnormal, schizophrenic, depressed, stupid, dishonest, crazy, lazy , cowardly, selfish, dull etc. until nothing but pleasant platitudes are heard and one is left puzzled as to who fills the jails, hospitals and mental wards to overflowing, litters the streets with garbage, destroys the parks, beaches and public lands, robs, riots, assaults, rapes and murders, and uses up all the tax money, plus an extra 2.5 billion dollars a day, added to the 18 trillion national debt (or over 90 trillion if you extend the real liabilities into the near future). Of course, it's not due all to the Diverse, but every passing day a larger percentage is.

It is now over fifty years after passing the new immigration act and about 15% of the population is Hispanic (up from less than 1% earlier), who have been reproducing at about 3X the rate of Euros , so that about half of children under 6 are now Hispanic, while some 13% of the country are blacks, rapidly being displaced and marginalized by Hispanics (though few blacks realize it, so they continue to support the politicians favoring further immigration and handouts and promising short term gains). Virtually nobody grasps the eventual collapse of America and the whole world, in spite of the fact that you can see it in front of your eyes everywhere. In America and worldwide, the Euros (and all the "rich" generally) are producing less than two kids per couple, so their populations are shrinking, and in America in 2014, for the first time since Euros came here, more of them died than were born, so their marginalization is certain. And, showing the "success" of the Democrats immigration and welfare policies, the population of Hispanics in California passed 50%, so within a decade, the 6th largest economy in the world will be part of Mexico.

The Diverse will, in, this century, eliminate all American "racism" (i.e., any opposition or legal hindrance to takeover of all political power, and the appropriation of as much of their neighbor's money and property as they can manage,) except their own racism (e.g., graduated income tax which forces the Euro's to support them). Soon they will largely eliminate legal differences between citizens of Mexico and California and then Texas, who then will have full 'rights' (privileges) anywhere in the USA, so that citizenship will became increasingly meaningless (and an ever-lower percentage of the Diverse will pay any significant taxes or serve in the military, and a far higher percentage will continue to receive welfare and to commit crimes, and to get free or heavily subsidized schooling, medical care etc.). One cannot mention in the media that the predominant racism in the USA is the extortion by the Diverse of anyone with money (mainly Euros but also any Diverse who have money), the elimination of free speech (except their own), the biasing of all laws to favor this extortion, and their rapid takeover of all political and financial power, i.e., total discrimination against Euros and anyone belonging to the "upper classes", i.e., anyone who pays any significant taxes.

Gradually the poverty, drugs, gangs, environmental destruction and the corruption of police, army and government endemic in Mexico and most other 3rd world countries is spreading across America, so we will be able to cross over the increasingly porous border with Mexico without noticing we are in a different country –probably within a few decades, but certainly by the end of the century. The population continues to increase, and here as everywhere in the world, the increase is now 100% Diverse and, as we enter the next century (much sooner in some countries), resources will diminish and starvation, disease, crime and war will rage out of control. The rich and the corporations will mostly still be rich (as always, as things get worse they will take their money and leave), the poor will be poorer and more numerous, and life everywhere, with the possible exception of a few countries or parts of countries where population growth is prevented, will be unbearable and unsurvivable.

The cooperation among the Diverse to wrest control of society from Euros will crumble as society disintegrates and they will split into blacks, Hispanics, Muslims, Chinese, Filipinos, gays, seniors, disabled, and further where possible into endless subgroups. The rich will increasingly hire bodyguards, carry guns, drive bulletproof cars and use private police to protect them in their gated communities and offices, as is already commonplace in 3rd world countries. With much reduced quality of life and high crime, some will think of returning to their countries of origin, but there also overpopulation will exhaust resources and produce collapse even more severe than in the USA and Europe, and the racism in the 3rd world, temporarily suppressed by a relative abundance of resources and police and military presence, will become ever worse, so life will be hellish nearly everywhere. The population in the 22nd century will shrink as billions die of starvation, disease, drugs, suicide, and civil and international war. As third world nuclear countries collapse (Pakistan, India and maybe Iran by then, thanks to Obama) and are taken over by radicals, nuclear conflicts will eventually occur. Still, perhaps nobody will dare to suggest publicly that the prime cause of chaos was unrestricted motherhood.

Of course, much of this story has already played out in America, the U.K. and elsewhere, and the rest is inevitable, even without climate change, which just makes it happen faster. It's only a matter of how bad it will get where and when. Anyone who doubts this is out of touch with reality, but you can't fool mother nature, and their descendants will no longer debate it as they will be forced to live it.

The poor, and apparently, Obama, Krugman, Zuckerberg and most Democrats, don't understand the most basic operating principle of civilization—there is no Free Lunch. You can only give to one by taking from another, now or in the future. No such thing as helping without hurting. Every dollar and every item has value because somewhere, someone destroyed the earth. And leftists have the delusion that they can solve all problems by stealing from the rich. To get some idea of the absurdity of this, all US taxpayers earning over a million have a total after tax profit of about 800 billion, while the annual deficit is about 1.5 trillion, and even taking it all does nothing to pay off the existing 18 trillion debt or the approx. 90 trillion in near term unfunded liabilities (e.g., medicare and social security). Of course, you cannot increase their tax or corporate tax very much more or it will greatly depress the economy and produce a recession, job losses and the flight of capital, and they already pay the highest taxes, relative to what they earn as a % of the nation's income, of any industrialized country. And once again, the top 1% of earners pay about 50% of total personal federal income tax while the bottom 40% (mostly Diverse) pay nothing. So the fact is we only have a sort of democracy, as we have almost nothing to say about what the govt. does, and a sort of fascism, as the ever expanding govt. spies on our every move, controls ever more minutely our every action, and forces us at gunpoint to do whatever they decide, and a sort of communism as they steal whatever they want from whomever they want and use it to support anyone they like, here and all over the world, most of whom have no interest in democracy, justice, or equality, except as means to take advantage of our fatally flawed system to get as much money and services as they can in order to support replicating their genes and destroying the earth.

Speaking of Obama, Trump says that he is the worst president ever, and of course Obama, totally arrogant, dishonest and lacking any real grasp of the situation (as usual for politicians) just laughs, and babbles platitudes, but as I reflect a bit it's clearly true. Like Roosevelt, who gave us the first giant step into fascism and govt. waste and oppression with an illegal and unconstitutional tax (social security), Obamacare let the govt. swallow 1/6 of the economy and created his own illegal tax (called 'penalties' of Obamacare, where FDR called them 'benefits' and 'contributions'). He tried to force the US to accept another 8 to 10 million illegals (nobody seems quite sure) which will 'birthright' into about 50 million by 2100. In the first 3 years of his office (2009 to 2012) the federal operating deficit increased about 44% from 10 to 15 trillion, the largest percent increase since WW2, while by mid 2015 it had increased to over 71% of fiscal operating budget -- over $18 trillion or about $57,000 for every person in the USA, including children. His deferral of the deportation of millions of illegals, all of whom now receive social security, tax credits, medicare etc., is estimated to have a lifetime cost to the govt. (i.e., to the minority of us who pay any significant taxes) of ca. $1.3 trillion. Of course, this does not include free school, use of judicial system, jails and police, free 'emergency' care (i.e., just going to emergency for any problem whatsoever), degradation of all public facilities etc. so it's likely at least twice as much. And we have seen 8 years of incompetent handling of the Iraq, Afghan and Syrian wars. Then he probably gave the ability to make nuclear weapons to Iran, which is highly likely to lead to a nuclear war by 2100 or much sooner. He was clearly elected for racist, third world supremacist reasons-- because he had visible African genes, while the Euros, having left Africa some 50,000 years earlier have invisible ones. He, and most of the people he appointed, had little competence or experience in running a country and they were picked, like himself, on the basis of Diverse genes and communist/fascist sympathies. If he is not a traitor (giving aid and comfort to the enemy) then who is? It is clear as day that, like nearly everyone, he operates totally on automatic primitive psychology, with his coalitional sympathies going to those who look and act more like him. He (like most Diverse) is in fact doing his best to destroy the country that made his exalted life possible. In an interview near the end of his term he said that the major reason for the backwardness of the third world was colonialism. As with all leftist third world supremacists, it has never crossed his mind that about 95% of all the third world people owe their existence and their relatively high standard of living to Euros and colonialism (i.e., medicine, agriculture, technology, science, trade, education, police and judicial system, communications, elimination of war and crime etc.), nor that the real enemies of the poor are other poor, who are just as repulsive as the rich, whom it is their greatest desire to emulate. I agree that, with the possible exception of Lincoln, he is the worst (i.e., most destructive to American quality of life and survival as a nation) for his lack of honesty, arrogance and assault on freedom and longterm survivability —a stunning achievement when his competition includes Nixon, Johnson and the Bushes.

When considering bad presidents, we should start with Abraham Lincoln, who is revered as a saint, but he (with the help of congress) destroyed much of the country and the lives of millions of people fighting the totally unnecessary Civil War, and in many ways, the country will never recover as it led to the civil rights movement, the 1965 immigration act and the 1982 supreme court anchor baby ruling. Slavery would have come to an end soon without the war, as it did everywhere and of course it was Euros who provided the main impetus to bring it to an end here and everywhere. After the war the slaves could have been repatriated to Africa, or just given residence, instead of making them citizens (14th amendment) and then giving them the vote (15th amendment). He and his collaborators, like so many liberal upper class Euros then and now, was blinded by the utopian social delusions embodied in Christianity and democracy, which result from the inclusive fitness psychology of coalitional intuitions and reciprocal altruism, that was eugenic and adaptive in the EEA (Environment of Evolutionary Adaptation-i.e., from ca. 50,000 to several million years ago) but is fatally dysgenic and maladaptive in modern times.

Note the great irony of the quote from him that begins this book, which shows that even the brightest are victims of their own limits, and have no grasp of human biology, psychology or ecology. It never crossed his mind that the world would become horrifically overpopulated and that the Africans would grow to become a giant social problem, at home and for themselves and the world as Africa expands to over 4 billion. Likewise, in spite of the now clear disaster, it seems not to cross Obama's that the Diverse will destroy America and the world, though any bright ten year old can see it.

President Truman could have let McArthur use the atom bomb to end the Korean war and to avoid the continuing horror of China. Johnson could have done likewise in Vietnam, Bush in Iraq and Obama in Afghanistan, Syria and Libya. Probably many 3rd world countries would have done so and almost certainly some of the Muslim ones in similar circumstances. Once a radical Muslim country gets the bomb a preemptive strike by them or on them will quickly ensue and this is likely by 2100 and near certain by 2200. If Gaddafi had succeeded in his efforts to get the bomb it would likely have already happened. The US could have forced Japan, China and Korea, Iraq and Libya and all the countries of Europe (and the whole world for that matter) to pay for the costs of our military efforts in all the recent wars, instead of taking on most of the cost and then helping them take over most of America's manufacturing. Of course these decisions , critical to the country's survival, were made by a handful of politicians without consulting the voters. The Kennedy's were an important part of changing the immigration laws in the mid 60's, so they have to count as traitors and major enemies of America on a par with Obama, G.W Bush and the Clintons. We could have followed the universal pleas of US industry and refused to sign the GATT, which gave free access to all our patents years before they are granted, though of course the Chinese now hack and steal everything with impunity anyway. Eisenhower could have let the UK keep possession of the Suez canal, instead of blackmailing them into leaving Egypt, and on and on.

Some may be interested in a few statistics to give an idea of where we currently are on the road to hell. See the tables at the beginning. In the USA, the population of Hispanics will swell from about 55 million in 2016 (or as much as 80 million if you accept some estimates of 25 million illegals—it's a mark of how far the govt. has let things go that we don't really know) to perhaps 140 million midcentury and 200 million as we enter the 22nd century, at which time the US population will be soaring past 500 million, and the world population will be about 11 billion, 3 billion of that added from now to then in Africa and 1 billion in Asia (the official UN estimates at the moment). The Hispanics are reproducing so fast that Euros, now a 63% majority, will be a minority by midcentury and about 40% by 2100. Most of the increase in the USA from now on will be Hispanics, with the rest blacks, Asians and Muslims, and all the increase here and in the world will be 100% Diverse. About 500,000 people are naturalized yearly and since they are mostly from the 3rd world and produce children at about twice the rate of Euros, that will add perhaps 2 million midcentury and 5 million by 2100 for every year it continues.

To show how fast things got out of control after the "no demographic impact" TKO (technical knock out or Ted Kennedy Outrage, though we could equally call it the LBJ outrage, the Democratic outrage, the Liberal outrage etc.) immigration act of 1965, there are now more Hispanics in California than there are people in 46 other states. In 1970 just after the TKO, there were about 4 million Hispanics and now there are over 55 million "legals" (i.e., not made legal by the voters but by a handful of politicians and the supremely stupid court) and perhaps 80 million counting illegals. It never crosses the minds of the Democratic block-voting poor Diverse that the ones who will suffer by far the most from the "Diversification" of America are themselves. The U.S. has gone from 84 percent white, 11 percent black, 4 percent Hispanic and 1 percent Asian in 1965, to 62 percent white, 11 percent black, 18 percent Hispanic and 6 percent Asian now, according to a recent Pew report. By 2055, no one group is expected to have a majority--a perfect scenario for chaos, but you can see countless idiots from academia praising multipartisanism. The Asians are predicted to increase faster than any group, doubling their percentage in the next few decades, but at least they will have gone thru a minimal immigration procedure, except of course for anchor baby families (producing which is now a major industry as Asians fly here to give birth, though they are greatly surpassed by Hispanics who only have to walk across the border at night). Of course, the Asians are by and large a blessing for America as they are more productive and less trouble than any group, including Euros.

The US government (alone of major countries) pushes "diversity" but in countries all over the world and throughout history attempts to weld different races and cultures into one have been an utter disaster. Many groups have lived among or alongside others for thousands of years without notably assimilating. Chinese and Koreans and Japanese in Asia, Jews and gentiles in thousands of places, Turks, Kurds and Armenians etc., have lived together for millennia without assimilating and go for each other's throats at the slightest provocation. After over 300 years of racial mixing, the USA is still about 97% monoracial (i.e., white, Hispanic, black etc.) with only about 3% describing themselves as mixed race (and most of them were mixed when they came here). The Native Americans (to whom the whole New World really belongs if one is going to rectify past injustices against the Diverse, a fact which is never mentioned by the third world supremacists) are mostly still living isolated and (before the casinos) impoverished, as are the blacks who, 150 years after emancipation, largely still live in crime ridden, impoverished ghettos. And these have been the best of times, with lots of cheap land and natural resources, major affirmative action programs (unique to 'racist' America), a mostly healthy economy and a government which extorts over 30% of their money (i.e., 30% of their working lives, counting income tax, sales tax, real estate tax etc.), earned by the tax paying part of the middle and upper class, to give the poor massive handouts -- not only food stamps and other welfare, but police and emergency services, streets and parks, the government, the justice system, hospitals, national defense, schools, roads, bridges, power grid, etc., and the costs of environmental degradation, and the financial and emotional costs of crime and it's threat, etc., most of these never counted by anyone (and never mentioned by third world supremacists) when considering the 'costs of welfare' or the huge downside to diversity.

In any case, the liberal, democratic delusion is that such largesse and social policies will weld our 'diverse' (i.e., fatally fragmented) society into one happy family. But government handouts need to continually increase (for social security, wars, health care, schools, welfare, infrastructure, etc.) while the relative tax base shrinks, and our debt and unfunded entitlements grow by trillions a year, so the economy is in the process of collapse. The average family has less real net earnings and savings now than two decades ago and could survive about 3 months without income, about 40% of retired Americans have less than $25,000 savings etc. And again, these are the best of times with lots of 'free' resources (i.e., stolen from others and from our descendants) worldwide and about 4 billion less people than there will be by the next century. As economies fail and starvation, disease, crime and war spread, people will split down racial and religious lines as always, and in the USA Hispanics and Blacks will still dominate the bottom. It rarely occurs to those who want to continue (and increase) the numbers of and the subsidization of the Diverse that the money for this is ultimately stolen from their own descendants, on whom falls the burden of over $90 trillion debt if one counts the current entitlements (or up to $220 trillion if liabilities continued without reduction of handouts and no tax increase), and a society and a world collapsing into anarchy.

As noted, one of the many evil side effects of diversity (e.g., massive increases in crime, environmental degradation, traffic gridlock, decreasing quality of schools, coming bankruptcy of local, state and federal governments, corruption of police and border officials, rising prices of everything, overloading of the medical system, etc.) is that our right to free speech has disappeared on any issue of possible political relevance and of course that means just about any issue. Even in private, if any negative comment on 'diversity' is recorded or witnessed by anyone credible, the racist, third world supremacist Diverse and their Euro servants will try to take away your job and damage your business or your person. This is certain when it involves public figures and racial or immigration issues, but nothing is off limits. Dozens of books in the last two decades address the issue including 'The New Thought Police: Inside the Left's Assault on Free Speech and Free Minds', 'End of Discussion: How the Left's Outrage Industry Shuts Down Debate, Manipulates Voters, and Makes America Less Free (and Fun)' and 'The Silencing: how the left is killing free speech', but nothing will dissuade the Democratic Socialists (i.e., closet communists) and the lunatic fringe liberals. As noted, I am writing this book because nobody in Academia, nor any public figure, dares to do it.

Another 'side effect' is the loss of much of our freedom and privacy as the government continues to expand its war on terror. There was never a compelling reason for admitting any serious number of Muslims (or any more Diverse for that matter). In any case, it seems a no-brainer to not admit and to expel single unmarried male Muslims aged 15 to 50, but even such obvious simple moves are beyond the capabilities of the retards who control congress and of course our beloved presidents, all of whom, with the members of congress, who voted for the immigration law changes starting in 1965, could be held personally responsible for 9/11, the Boston Marathon Bombing etc. Of course, Trump is trying to change this but it's too little, too late and barring his declaring martial law, running the country with the army, and deporting or quarantining 100 million of the least useful residents, America's date with destiny is certain.

A lovely example of how suppression of free speech leads to ever more insanity is the case of Major Hasan (courtesy Mark Steyn's "After America"). An army psychiatrist at Fort Hood who had SoA (Soldier of Allah) on his business card, he was frequently reprimanded when a student army intern for trying to convert patients to Islam, and many complaints were filed for his constant anti-American comments--one day he gave a Power Point lecture to a room full of army doctors justifying his radicalism. Free speech and common sense being no more available in the military than civilian life, he was then promoted to Major and sent to Fort Hood, where he commented to his superior officer on a recent murder of two soldiers in Little Rock: "this is what Muslims should do—stand up to the aggressors" and "people should strap bombs on themselves and go into Times Square", but the army did nothing for fear of being accused of bias. One day he walked out of his office with an assault rifle and murdered 13 soldiers. It turned out two different anti-terrorism task forces were aware that he had been in frequent email contact with top radical Islamist terrorists. The Army Chief of Staff General George Casey remarked: "What happened at Fort Hood was a tragedy, but I believe it would be an even greater tragedy if our diversity becomes a casualty here"!! Is it losing the 70 million on welfare or the 1.7 million in prison or the 3 million drug addicts that is more tragic?

The invasion of the Southwest by Hispanics gives the flavor of what is coming and Coulter in her book "Adios America" tells of trashed parks, schools that dropped from A to D grade, billions for 'free' (i.e., paid for by the upper middle and upper class and businesses) medical care and other services in Los Angeles alone etc. Anyone living there who remembers what Texas or California were like 30 years ago has no doubts about the catastrophic consequences of diversity as they see it every day. In California, which I know personally, the urban areas (and even most parks and beaches) that I used to enjoy are now crowded with Hispanics and often full of trash and spray painted with gang signs, while the highways are horrifically crowded and the cities and towns overrun with drugs and crime, so most of it is now uninhabitable and the world's 6th largest economy is headed for bankruptcy as it tries to move 20 million mostly lower class Hispanics into the upper middle class by using tax money from the Euros. One of the latest lunacies was to try to put all illegals on Obamacare. Some persons I know have had their annual medical coverage increase from under $1000 before Obamacare to about $4000 (2017 estimate) and the extra $3000 is what the Democrats are stealing from anyone they can to cover the costs of free or very low cost care for those who pay little or no taxes, and who already are bankrupting hospitals forced to give them free "emergency" care. Of course, the Republicans are trying to kill it, but like the whole government, it is already in a death spiral that only a huge increase in fees can fix.

One of the most flagrant violations of US law by the left-wing lunatics who support immigration is the creation of 'sanctuary cities'. The cities do not allow municipal funds or resources to be used to enforce federal immigration laws, usually by not allowing police or municipal employees to inquire about an individual's immigration status. This began with Los Angeles in 1979 (thus becoming the first large city donated to Mexico) and now includes at least 31 major American cities. Presumably, the President could order the army or the FBI to arrest the city officials who passed these regulations for obstruction of justice etc., but it's a murky legal area as (in another indication of the total ineptness of congress and the courts and the hopelessness of the democratic system) immigration violations are civil offenses and not federal or state felonies which they clearly should be. After I wrote this the courts (predictably) blocked Trump's attempt to cut off funds to sanctuary cities, forgetting that their purpose is to protect the citizens of America, and not those of other countries here illegally. And recently California declared itself a sanctuary state, i.e., it's now part of Mexico.

A competent government (maybe we could import one from Sweden, China or even Cuba?) could pass such legislation in a few weeks. Also, it could force compliance by cutting off most or all federal funds to any city or state that failed to comply with federal immigration laws, and at least one such bill has been introduced into congress recently, but the Democrats prevented its passage, and of course Obama or Clinton would have vetoed any attempt at giving American back to Americans. Trump of course has a different view, though he cannot save America via democratic means.

As long as the Democrats (soon to return to power and, rumor has it, to change their name to Socialist Democratic Communist Third World Supremacist Party of Latin America, Asia, Africa and the Middle East) are in power, nothing will be done, and more cities and states will cease to be a part of America until Hispanics take over completely sometime in the second half of the century. Only a military coup can save America now and it's very unlikely the generals have the courage.

For this review, I read a few politically oriented books and articles in print and on the web of the kind that I have avoided for over 50 years, and in them and the comments on them saw repeated accusations of 'racist' against people who were only stating their desire to have the USA remain a prosperous and safe country. This claim is now almost always false in the normal meaning, but of course true in the new meaning—i.e., one opposed to letting Mexico and Africa annex America. So, I wrote a reply to this slander, since I have never seen a good one.

Actually, it's not 'racism' but self-defense –the Diverse in America are the racists, as on the average, your life here is largely an exploitation of other races, notably Europeans and Asians who actually pay taxes. For genuine racism look at how different groups native to your own country or immigrants are treated there. The vast majority of immigrants in the USA would not even be permitted to enter your countries, much less permitted citizenship, the privilege of voting, free or low cost housing, food, free of subsidized medical care, free school, affirmative action programs, the same privileges as natives etc. And in the USA, it is the Diverse who have taken away the tranquility, beauty, safety and free speech that existed here before a handful of stupid politicians and supreme court justices let you in. We never voted to let you enter or become citizens--it was forced on us by halfwits in our government, beginning with Lincoln and his partners in crime. If we had a chance to vote on it, few foreigners except medical, scientific and tech experts and some teachers would have been admitted and perhaps 75% of the Diverse would be deported. In many cases, you have an alien religion (some of which demand the murder of anyone you take a dislike to) and culture (honor killings of your daughters etc.), do not pay a fair share of taxes (typically none) and commit far more crimes per capita (e.g., 2.5x for Hispanics, 4.5x for blacks).

Furthermore, the middle class American pays about 30% of their income to the govt. This is about 66 days/year of their working life and maybe 20 days of that goes to support the poor, now mostly Diverse. And all the 'free' things such as welfare, food stamps, medical care and hospitals, schools, parks, streets, sanitation, police, firemen, power grid, postal system, roads and airports, national defense etc. exist largely because the 'racist' upper middle and upper class created, maintain and pay for them. Maybe another 4 working days goes to support the police, FBI, justice system, DHS, Border Patrol and other govt. agencies that have to deal with aliens. Add another 10 or so days to support the military, which is mostly needed to deal with the results of 3rd world overpopulation (the real major cause of the Korean War, the Vietnam War, Iraq, Afghanistan, Syria, Libya, Yemen and the major cause of most of the wars, social unrest and conflicts past, present and future), and this cost, added to welfare, medicare, social security and environmental degradation (an ever increasing percentage for immigrants and their descendants) is bankrupting the country, with the only possible solution being to decrease the benefits and increase the taxes, the burden of which will fall on everyone's descendants. You take advantage of the freedom of speech we created to tell malicious lies about us and prevent rational discussion! Most of you, if doing this in your country of origin, would wind up in prison or dead! Shameless liars! What is your problem? --poor education, no gratitude, malicious, stupid, no experience with civilized society? (pick 5).

And anyone who doubts any of this just does not know how to use their brain or the net as it's all there. These comments are just the facts that anyone can see, along with simple extrapolations into the future.

Also, please let me ask the Diverse--do people in your country of origin work 30 days a year to support tens of millions of aliens who commit crimes at several times the rate of natives, overcrowd your schools, highways, cities and jails, trash your parks and beaches, spray paint graffiti on buildings and import and sell drugs to addicts who commit over a hundred million crimes a year (added to the 100 million or so they commit themselves)? And have you had a 9/11 and many bombings and murders at home? Do immigrants control the media so that you cannot even discuss these issues that are destroying your country and the world? Will your country be totally in their control in a few generations and be another impoverished, crime ridden, starving, corrupt 3rd world hellhole? Of course, for most of you it already is, and you came to America to escape it. But your descendants won't have to be homesick for the hellhole, as they will have re-created it here. The Diverse here (and their Euro servants) never tire of complaining in all the media every day about how they are not treated fairly and not given enough (i.e., the Euros and the relatively rich Diverse don't work hard enough to support them), and it never crosses their minds that if it were not for taxes paid mostly by Euros now and for over a century previous, there would be little or no police or fire or medical or school services or parks or public transport or streets or sewers in their communities, and of course there would not even be a country here, as it is mainly Euros who created, and support it and who serve in the military in all the wars. And it was primarily Euros and their descendants who created the net and the pc's that was used to create this and the electronic or print media you are reading this on, the tech that produces the food you eat and the medicine that keeps you alive. If not for the Euros technology and security, at least 90% of all the Diverse in the world would not exist. Everyone condemns colonialism, but it was the way that the Diverse were brought out of the dark ages into modern times via communications, medicine, agriculture, and enforcement of democratic government. Otherwise all their populations would have stayed very small, backwards, starving, disease ridden, impoverished, isolated and living in the dark ages (including slavery and its equivalents) to this day. To sum it up, the Euro's antipathy to Diversity ('racism') is due to a desire that their children have a country and a world worth living in. Again, this is for everyone's benefit, not just Euros or the rich.

Likewise, all my life I have been hearing third world people saying that their disproportionate problems with drugs, crime and welfare are due to racism, and certainly there is some truth to that, but I wonder why Asians, who must be subject to racism as well (insofar as it exists — and relative to most Diverse counties, it's quite minimal here), and most of whom came here much more recently, spoke little or no English, had no relatives here and few skills, have a fraction of the crime, drugs and welfare (all less than Euros and so way less than blacks or Hispanics) and average about $10,000 more income per family than Euros. Also, blacks never consider that they would not exist if their ancestors were not brought to the new world and they would never have been born or survived in Africa, that those who captured and sold them were usually African, that to this day Africans in Africa almost universally treat those of different tribes as subhuman (Idi Amin, Rwanda, Gaddafi etc. and far worse is soon to come as the population of Africa swells by 3 billion by 2100), and that if they want to see real racism and economic exploitation and police maltreatment, they should go live almost anywhere in Africa or the 3rd world. Returning to Africa or Mexico etc. has always been an option, but except for criminals escaping justice, nobody goes back. And it was the Euros who put an end to slavery worldwide and, insofar as possible, to serfdom, disease, starvation, crime and war all over the 3rd world. If it were not for colonialism and the inventions of Euros there would be maybe 1/10 as many Diverse alive and they would mostly still be living as they did 400 years ago. Likewise, it's never mentioned that if not for the Euro's, who were about 95% responsible for paying for and fighting and dying in WW2, the Germans and Japanese and/or the Communists would now control the world. Also, it was mostly Euro's who fought, are fighting and will be fighting the communists in Korea and Vietnam, and the Muslim fanatics in Iraq, Syria, Libya and Afghanistan and the many others soon to come.

Insofar as any revenge is needed for their slavery, blacks have already had it abundantly. First, they have been largely supported and protected by the Euros for centuries. Second, the parasites they brought with them have infected and destroyed the lives of tens of millions of Euros. Malaria, schistosomes, filariasis, ascaris, yellow fever, smallpox etc., but above all hookworm, which was so common and so debilitating up to the early decades of this century that it was responsible for the widespread view of Southerners as stupid and lazy.

All this is crushingly obvious, but I bet there is not one grade school or college text in the world that mentions any of it, as it's clearly 'racist' to suggest that the Diverse owe anything to Euros or to point out that other Diverse treat them far worse than Euros. And they are incapable of grasping the true horror that is coming or they would all be one in opposing any increase in the population by any group anywhere and any immigration into America. Well before 2100 the Hispanics will control America, and increasingly the world will be dominated by Muslims, who will increase from about 1/5th of the world now to about 1/3rd by 2100 and outnumber Christians, and neither group is noted for embracing multiculturalism. So, the obvious fact is that overall the Euros have treated the Diverse much better than they have treated each other. And we now have the best of times, while by 2100 (give or take a generation or two) economic collapse and chaos will reign permanently except perhaps a few places that forcibly exclude Diverse. Again, keep in mind that in my view there is not, and almost certainly will never be, any evidence of a significant genetic difference between Euros and Diverse in psychology, or IQ, and that their tendency to excessive reproduction and other cultural limitations are accidents of history.

Likewise, it never crosses their minds that every year maybe 500 billion dollars are spent by federal, state and city govts. on education, medicine, transportation (highways, streets, rail, bus and airline systems), police, fire and emergency care, numerous welfare programs, the government and judicial systems--the vast majority of it created, maintained and paid for by the Euros, assisted by the taxes of the small minority of well-off Diverse. Also, there is the FBI, NSA, CIA, and the armed forces of the USA (another 500 billion a year) and other Euro countries, without which there would be no USA and little or no peace, security or prosperity anywhere in the world, and they have also been created, run and staffed largely by the Euros, who constitute most of the dead and wounded in every war (less an issue for Hispanics who serve in the military at about half the rate of Euros) and in every police force from 1776 to now. Without medicine and public health measures, most of their ancestors (and the whole third world) would have suffered and often died of leprosy, malaria, worms, bacteria, flu, tuberculosis, smallpox, syphilis, HIV, hepatitis, yellow fever, encephalitis, and the tech for high cholesterol and blood pressure, heart, cancer, and liver surgery, MRI, XRAY, Ultrasound etc., etc., has almost all been invented, administered and overwhelmingly paid for by the Euro 'racists' and 'white supremacists'.

You think colonialism was bad? Just think what the 3rd world would be like without it, or what it would be like living under the Nazis, communists or Japanese (and will be like living under the Chinese once the Diverse destroy America). This excuses nothing but just points out the facts of history. But fine, let's undo the 'injustice' and pass a Back to Africa (and Latin America and Asia etc.) law providing funds to repatriate everyone. They could sell their assets here and most could live like kings there, but of course there would be very few takers. And by the next century there will be 3 billion more Africans (the official estimate) and the whole continent will be a sewer, and 1 billion more Asians, and even India and China (who will add a few hundred million each) will look like paradise in comparison to Africa, at least until the resources run out (oil, gas, coal, topsoil, fresh water, fish, minerals, forests).

If you look on the net you find the Diverse incessantly whining about their oppression, even when it occurred decades or centuries ago, but I don't see how anything that's done by others, even today, is my responsibility, and much less so in the past. If you want to hold every Euro responsible for what the vast majority now alive are completely innocent of, then we want to hold all Diverse responsible for all the crimes committed by any of them here over the last 400 years, and for their share of all the tens of trillions we spent to build and defend the USA and to keep them safe, healthy and well fed. Yes, most blacks and Hispanics are poor due to historical factors beyond their control, just as Euros are often richer due to historical factors beyond theirs, but the important points are that we now alive did not cause this, and that here, as almost everywhere that the Diverse are a significant percentage, they commit most of the crime, collect most of the welfare, pay the least taxes and continue breeding excessively and dragging their countries and the world into the abyss.

Consider as well that the evils of colonialism are only prominent because they were recent. If we look carefully, we find that nearly every group in every country has an endless history of murder, rape, plunder and exploitation of their neighbors that continues today. It's not far off the mark to suggest that the best thing that could happen was to be conquered by the Euros.

Once again, keep in mind that there is not and almost certainly will never be any evidence of a significant genetic difference between Euros and Diverse and that their limitations are almost certainly due to culture. The problem is not the Diverse nor Euros, but that people are selfish, stupid, dishonest, lazy, crazy, and cowardly and will only behave decently, honestly, and fairly if forced to do so. Giving people rights instead of having privileges they must earn is a fatal mistake that will destroy any society and any world. In the tiny groups in which we evolved, where everyone was our relative, reciprocal altruism worked, but in a world soon swelling to 11 billion, this impulse to help others is suicidal. The world is totally preoccupied with terrorists, but their effects are actually trivial compared e.g., to traffic accidents, murders, drug addiction, disease, soil erosion etc., and every day the 7.7 billion do vastly more damage to the world just by living. The mothers of the third world increase the population by about 200,000 every day, and so do hugely more damage every hour than all the terrorists worldwide will do in the whole 21st century (until they get their hands on the bomb). Just the Diverse in the USA in one year will do far more damage to the USA and the world by destroying resources, eroding topsoil and creating CO2 and other pollution than all terrorism worldwide in all of history. Is there even one politician or entertainer or business person who has a clue? And if they did would they say or do anything— certainly not—who wants to be attacked for 'racism'.

People everywhere are lazy, stupid and dishonest and democracy, justice and equality in a large Diverse welfare state are an open invitation to limitless exploitation of their neighbors and few will resist. In 1979 7% of Americans got means-tested govt. benefits while in 2009 it was over 30% and of course the increase is mostly the diverse. Food stamps rose from 17 million persons in 2000 to about 43 million now. In the first few years of Obama over 3 million enrolled to get 'disability' checks and over 20% of the adult population is now on 'disability' which according to the Census Bureau includes categories such as "had difficulty finding a job or remaining employed "and "had difficulty with schoolwork". There are now almost 60 million working age (16 to 65) adults who are not employed or about 40% of the labor force. Illegal families get about $2.50 in direct benefits for every dollar they pay in taxes and about another $2.50 indirect benefits (and not counting their damage to the biosphere) so they are a huge and ever increasing drain in spite of frequent fake 'news stories' on the net about their great value.

Interest payments on our national debt are projected to rise to 85% of our total federal income by 2050. About half of our debt is owned by foreign govts., about a quarter by China, and if China continues to buy our debt at current rates, very soon our interest payments to them will cover their total annual military budget (ca. 80 billion vs U.S. of ca $600 billion) and (depending on interest rates) in a few years they would be able to triple or quadruple their military expenditures and it would all be paid for by US taxpayers. Actually, I have not seen it noted, but their lower costs mean that they are actually spending maybe 300 billion. And it is rarely mentioned why the US military budget is so enormous, and how it ties into the high life style and huge govt. subsidies in Europe and worldwide for that matter. The USA is the world's free policeman, providing technology, money and troops for keeping the peace and fighting wars worldwide and is too stupid to ask the other countries to pay their share--until the recent comments by Trump. To a significant extent, the ability of the Europeans and countries worldwide to have a high standard of living is due to the American taxpayers (without of course being asked) paying for their defense for the last 75 years.

The CIS reports total immigration will reach about 51 million by 2023, about 85% of the total population increase (all the rest due to the Diverse already here) and will soon comprise about 15% of the total population—by far the largest percentage in any big country in recent history. It was reported that the Dept. of Homeland Security New Americans Taskforce was directed to process the citizenship applications of the 9 million green card holders ASAP to try to influence the 2016 election.

The federal govt. is a cancer which now takes about 40% of all income from the minority who pay significant taxes and federal govt. civilian employees are hugely overpaid, averaging ca. $81,000 salary and $42,000 benefits while private employees get about $51,000 salary and $11,000 benefits. About 25% of all the goods and services produced in the USA are consumed by the govt. and about 75% of total govt. income is given out as business and farm subsidies and welfare. If all federal taxes were increased by 30% and spending was not increased, the budget might balance in 25 years. Of course, the spending would increase immediately if more money was available, and also the economy would take a huge hit as there would be less incentive to earn or to stay in the USA and business investment and earnings would drop. It is estimated that private sector compliance with govt. regulations costs about 1.8 trillion a year or about 12% of our total GDP, and of course it is growing constantly, so we waste more on govt. paperwork every year than the GDP of most countries. The main push for evermore confiscation of our money (years of our working lives) by the govt. is the communism/socialism/fascism forced on us by the rapid increase of Diverse, but being the world's police force for free has cost us trillions, which also translates into years of our working lives as detailed elsewhere here.

The poor are almost always spoken of as though they were somehow superior to the rich and it is implicit that we ought to make sacrifices for them, but they are only the rich in waiting and when they get rich they are inevitably exactly as loathsome and exploitative. This is due to our innate psychology, which in the small groups in which we evolved made sense, as everyone was our relative, but in a world that is fast collapsing due to the expansion of the Diverse it makes no sense. The poor care no more about others than the rich.

Marvelous that even Obama and the Pope speak about the coming horrors of climate change, but of course not a word about the irresponsible motherhood that is its cause. The most you get from any govt. official, academic or TV documentary is a meek suggestion that climate change needs to be dealt with, but rarely a hint that overpopulation is the source of it and that most of it for the last century and all of it from now on is from the 3rd world. China now creates twice the C02 of the USA and USA Diverse create about 20% of USA pollution, which will rise to about 50% by the next century.

Ann Coulter in "Adios America" describes the outrageous story of what seems to be the only occasion on which Americans actually got to vote on the immigration issue—what some call "the great Prop 187 democracy ripoff".

In 1994 Californians, outraged to see ever more Hispanics crowding into the state and using up tax money, put on the ballot Proposition 187 which barred illegals from receiving state money. In spite of the expected opposition and outrageous lies from all the self-serving, boot licking Democrats and other left wingers, it passed overwhelmingly winning 2/3 of white, 56% of black, 57% of Asian and even 1/3 of Hispanic votes (yes, many middle and upper class Hispanics realize being taken over by Mexico will be a disaster). Note that all these people are 'racists' or 'white supremacists' (or in slightly more polite columns of the Carlos Slim Helu controlled NY Times etc. 'bigots' or 'nativists') according to the current use of this word by a large percentage of liberals, many Hispanics, the Sierra Club, the ACLU and even Nobel Prize winning economist Paul Krugman (who recently called Trump a 'racist' for daring to tell the truth while defending the USA from annexation by Mexico).

It even carried the hopeless Republican candidate for Governor, Pete Wilson to a landslide victory, with 1/3 of his voters stating his support for Prop 187 was their reason for voting for him. However, the "ACLU and other anti-American groups" (Coulter) brought suit and it was soon struck down by a Democratic appointed (i.e., 'honorary Mexican') District Court Judge for being unconstitutional (i.e., protecting Americans rather than aliens). As with the 1898 and 1982 Supreme Court decisions giving citizenship to anyone who is born here, it was another hallucinatory interpretation of our laws and a clear demonstration of the hopelessness of the court system, or any branch of the government (at least a Democrat dominated one) in protecting Americans from a third world takeover. It has been suggested that the ACLU change its name to the Alien Civil Liberties Union and that it, along with the many other organizations and individuals working to destroy the USA, be forced to register as agents of a foreign government or preferably, be classified as terrorists and all their employees and donors deported or quarantined.

In spite of this, neither the state nor federal govt. has done anything whatsoever to prevent the takeover, and Coulter notes that when G.W. Bush ran for president, he campaigned in America with the corrupt Mexican president Gortari (see comments on Carlos Slim below), had brother Jeb 'Illegal Immigration is an act of love' Bush speak in Spanish at the Republican National Convention, and after winning, gave weekly radio addresses in Spanish, added a Spanish page to the White House website, held a huge Cinco de Mayo party at the White House, and gave a speech to the blatantly racist National Council of La Raza, in which, among other outrages, he promised $100 million in federal money (i.e., our money) to speed immigration applications! Clearly with both the Republican and Democratic parties seeking annexation by Mexico, there is no hope for the democratic process in America unless it is drastically changed.

California is the 6th largest in economy in the world, ahead of France, Brazil, Italy, South Korea, Australia, Spain, India, Russia, and Canada, and more than double that of Mexico, and in about 10 years, when their 10 million kids grow up and the total Hispanic population of Calif is about 22 million (counting only legals), they will own the state and it will have been annexed by Mexico.

In recent years, Calif. Governor Brown signed legislation granting drivers licenses to illegals, and paying for free medical care for their children (i.e., of course we the taxpayers pay). He agreed to let noncitizens monitor polls for elections, and they have been appointed to other government positions such as city councils without state govt. approval. He also forced all state officials to commit obstruction of justice by signing a law known as the Trust Act (i.e., trust they won't rob, rape, murder, sell drugs etc.), which specifies that unless immigrants have committed certain serious crimes, they cannot be detained (for delivery to the feds for deportation) past when they would otherwise become eligible for release. The batch of new "lets become part of Mexico" laws also included one that would allow immigrants without legal status to be admitted to the state bar and practice law in California. But he vetoed the bill allowing illegal aliens to serve on juries. So, the only thing that prevented the final step in turning over the Calif. Courts to Mexico was the arbitrary decision of one man! However, it won't be more than a few years before an Hispanic is Governor and then this and endless other atrocities will ensue, including presumably giving illegals the right to vote perhaps by passing another state law that violates or obstructs the federal one. In any case, there will soon by little distinction in California between being a citizen of the USA and a citizen of any other country who can sneak across the border. Note that as usual the Citizens of California were never permitted to vote on any of these issues, which were passed by the Democratic controlled state legislature. Why don't they just be honest and change the name to Democratic Party of Mexico? At least they should be forced to register as the agent of a foreign govt.

It is certain that California (and by the end of the century the USA) is lost to civilization (i.e., it will be like Mexico, which of course will be far worse by then) unless the govt. sends federal troops into California (and other states with sanctuary cities) to deport illegals and arrest all those (including numerous elected officials) who are violating federal law. Even this will only slow up the catastrophe unless a law is passed terminating anchor babies (i.e., those getting citizenship because they are born here), preferably retroactively to 1982 or better to 1898, and rescinding citizenship for them and preferably all those who gained it from them—i.e. all their descendants and relatives. Also of course the 1965 immigration law must be declared unconstitutional and all those (and relatives and descendants) who immigrated since then have their status reviewed with the significant taxpayers remaining and the non or low payers repatriated. Hard to get precise statistics, as its 'racist' to even think about it, but in Stockton, California and Dallas, Texas about 70% of all births are to illegals and maybe 90% of the total counting all Hispanics, and of course the bills are almost all paid by Euros and 'rich' Diverse via forced taxation, which of course they never get to vote on.

To end birthright, a new law has to be passed and not an old one repealed, as there is no such law— this was an utterly arbitrary opinion of Justice Willie, "anchor baby" Brennan and only a handful of justices ever voted for this hallucinatory interpretation of the law. Those who want to see how the Supreme Court destroyed our country by eroding the boundary between being an American citizen and a person who was passing through (and the lack of basic common sense in the law and the hopelessness of the American legal system- and the contrary opinions of legal experts) can consult Levin's 'Men in Black' or see United States v. Wong Kim Ark, 169 U.S. 649 (1898)(yes it was a Chinese who began the assault on America over a century ago) where 6 lawyers (i.e., justices of the court) granted citizenship to the children of resident aliens and Plyler v. Doe, 457 U.S. 202 (1982) where 5 lawyers (with 4 disagreeing) granted citizenship to the children of illegal aliens and anyone giving birth while visiting. If just one of the 5 morons who voted for this had changed their mind we would have maybe 10 million fewer on the welfare rolls now and perhaps 50 million fewer by 2100. Of course, none of the other 450 million or so adults alive between then and now have ever been permitted to vote on this or any of the basic issues leading inexorably to collapse. As we now see in the media every day, in a 'representative' democracy what is represented is not America's interests, but egomania, greed, stupidity and third world supremacism.

How many people did it take to hand America to Mexico? For the TKO Immigration disaster in 1965 there were 320 representatives and 76 senators, and for anchor babies the two Supreme Court decisions totaling 11 lawyers, most of these 'outstanding citizens' now dead, so out of the approx. 245 million adult Americans citizens alive now, about 120 very senior citizens actually voted for the handover. As clear a demonstration of the hopelessness of representative democracy (as practiced here) as one could want.

Clearly, if America is to remain a decent place to live for anyone, the 1965 act, and all subsequent ones, need to be repealed by a law that puts a moratorium on all immigration and naturalization, and preferably rescinds or at least reviews citizenship for everyone naturalized since 1965 (or preferably since the first absurd birthright ruling in 1898), along with all their relatives and descendants. All their cases could be reviewed and citizenship conferred on select individuals who scored high enough on a point scale, with welfare recipients, the chronically unemployed, felons, and their descendants ineligible, those with college or medical degrees, teachers, engineers, business owners etc., getting points towards eligibility, i.e., just basic common sense if America is to survive.

Following Ann Coulter ('Adios America'), we note that corporate tax in the USA is the highest in the world at 39% and as the govt. continues to raise taxes to support the half of the country that is on some kind of welfare (if one includes social security, unemployment, food stamps, housing subsidies, welfare and veterans benefits), inevitably capital and jobs will leave, and entering the next century with vanishing resources, and since the entire annual population increase of 2.4 million is now Diverse, that means about 200 million more of them (for a total of around 350 million out of about 500 million) by 2100, a fragmented populace fighting for resources, and a drastically reduced standard of living with eventual collapse is inevitable.

Regarding the tax situation, in 2013, those with gross incomes above $250,000 (nearly all of them Euros) paid nearly half (48.9%) of all individual income taxes, though they accounted for only 2.4% of all returns filed and their average tax rate was 25.6%. The bottom 50% of filers (those making under $34,000-maybe half Diverse and half Euros) paid an average of 1.2% federal income tax for total share of 2.4% while the next 35% of filers (those making

$34k to $69k) averaged 21% tax rate for a total share of 10.5% of total federal income tax collected. So, it is obvious that contrary to the common view of the democrats/third world supremacists/communists,multiethnicists, the upper and upper middle class are giving the poor a largely free ride, and that we already have one foot in communism. However, we must not forget the $2.5 billion a day the US is going into debt and the total $80 trillion or more unfunded liabilities (e.g., social security and medicare), which will have to eventually be paid by some combo of increased taxes and decreased benefits to their descendants. Consider this: "When we combine the populations of non-payers and non-filers and look to see what overall percentage of each group is not paying taxes, we find that: 50.7 percent of African American households pay no income taxes, 35.5 percent of Asian American households do not, 37.6 percent of White American households do not, and 52 percent of (legal) Hispanics pay no income taxes." There are about 5X as many Euros (whites) as blacks and 4X as many whites as Hispanics in the USA, and there are about the same % of whites and blacks on welfare (39%) and about 50% of Hispanics, so percentage wise that means blacks are about 5X and Hispanics about 8X as likely to be on welfare as whites.

Including property taxes, sales taxes etc. brings the average middle class ($34k to $69k income) tax up to about 30%, so 4 months/year or about 15 years labor in a 50 year lifetime goes to the government, a large percentage to support immigrants who are destroying America and the world, and another large percentage for the military, which is a free police force for the rest of the world.

Counting all support as enumerated above (i.e., not just food stamps etc., but the poor's fair share of all other expenses) the average middle class family works roughly 5 weeks/year or 5 years of their working life to support the poor. Neither mass immigration, nor slavery, nor anchor babies, nor excessive breeding, nor unemployment, nor crimes and drugs are their fault, but the middle and upper class pay for the poor, and their kids will pay more (likely at least 10 years of their 50 year working life well before 2100) until the standard of living and quality of life is about the same as that of Diverse countries, and they will both drop continually every year until collapse.

Of course, every statistic has a counter statistic, but as a rough guide we find a recent study that found that 37% of Hispanic immigrant households got the majority of their income from welfare while 17% of blacks did (whites were not reported but I would guess about 10%). Of the $ 3.5 trillion budget, about 595 billion is deficit and about 486 billion goes to welfare, so eliminating welfare would almost balance it and eliminating all the costs associated with persons and their descendants naturalized since 1965 would put the USA solidly in the black and would probably allow paying off the $18 trillion national debt before the end of the century, while implementing a Naturalized Citizens Repatriation Act would likely allow this closer to midcentury.

As I write this I see a 'news item' (i.e., one of the endless barrage of paid lies planted there every day by the Diverse) on Yahoo that tells me that illegals are doing us a big favor as the majority are working and pay about $1000 each tax per year. But they don't tell us that they cost the country maybe $25,000 each in direct traceable costs and if you add their share of all the other costs (to maintain the govt. the police, the courts, the army, the streets etc., etc.) it's likely double that. As Coulter tells you on p47 of Adios America, a college educated person pays an average $29k taxes more per year than they get back in govt. services. Legal immigrants however get back an average $4344 more than they pay, while those without a high school degree get back about $37k more than they pay. She says that about 71% of illegal households get welfare.

About 20% of US families get 75% of their income from the govt. and another 20% get 40%. In the UK, which is about on a par with the USA on its Diverse path to ruin, about 5 million persons or 10% of able adults live totally on welfare and have not worked a day since the Labour govt. took over in 1997, and another 30% receive partial support. Greece, famous for it's recent huge bailout, is a typical case of how the masses always drag a country into chaos if permitted. People normally retire on full govt. pensions in their 50's and as early as 45, and when retirement at 50 was permitted for a couple of hazardous jobs like bomb disposal, it soon was enlarged to cover over 500 occupations including hairdressers (hazardous chemicals like shampoo) and radio and TV announcers (bacteria on microphones)—no I am not joking.

People often praise European countries for their generous welfare, but in fact it is mainly possible because nearly all their defense since the 50's (to say nothing about the two world wars), i.e., about $10 trillion in direct costs and perhaps another $10 trillion indirect) has been paid for by the USA, i.e., by the 20% of US taxpayers who pay any significant tax, plus much of the $18 trillion debt. In fact, like all the world, they would not even be independent countries if not for the USA who defeated the Germans in two wars and the Japanese and kept the communists under control for half a century. So not only is the U.S. bled dry by the poor and Diverse here, but we pay for them all over the world as well as helping the rich there get richer. Typical of all

Europe, in France, where the Muslims have become a huge problem, even when not slaughtering people, most of them are on welfare, paid for in part by the USA. For about a decade the biggest voting bloc in the U.N is the Organization of Islamic Cooperation which controls e.g., the Human Rights Council, where they allow only the rights permitted by Islamic law, and so forget women's rights, children's rights, gay rights, freedom of religion, free speech etc. and in fact freedom of any kind. As the muslims unrestrained breeding increases their percent of world population from 1/5 to 1/3 by 2100 or so, this will get much worse.

Islam is defended with such ferocity because in the poor 3rd world countries it has been the only defense against selfishness and it provides poor men with a guarantee of reproduction and survival. The same used to be the case for Christianity. It is also clear that as the 22nd century approaches and America collapses, China will replace it as the 'Great Satan' since it will be dominant worldwide, protecting its ever-growing investments and Chinese citizens, and eventually doing whatever it wants, as 'Diversification' results in control of America by Mexicans and Africans and it loses military superiority and the money and will to fight. And of course, the Chinese will not follow America's path and be 'diversified' into collapse, unless via some great misfortune they become democratic.

A bit off the mark but too nice to pass up is a lovely example of devolution (dysgenics) that is second only to overpopulation in bringing about the collapse of industrial civilization (though political correctness forbids discussion anywhere). U.K. Pakistanis, who often import their cousins to marry and so are inbreeding with up to 5 children a family, sometimes with multiple wives, produce 30% of the rare diseases in the UK, though they are 2% of the population. Of course, most are on welfare and the defectives result in huge expenses for full time nursing care and special education (for those not deaf and blind). And the European High Court ruled the govt must pay full spousal benefits to all the wives and can't draw the line at two.

A good part of Coulter's book is spent on crime, and we should first note (Coulter does not seem to, though I expect she knows) that it is rarely considered that it is hugely underreported, especially among the poor and Diverse. Thus, the BJS says that about 3.4 million violent crimes per year go unreported and the figures for nonviolent ones (burglary, assault, petty theft, vandalism, drug dealing, etc.) must be in the hundreds of millions, disproportionately committed by (and suffered by) the Diverse. One finds that the percent of adult males incarcerated for whites is 0.7, for Hispanics 1.5

and for blacks 4.7. It appears impossible to find any precise national figures for the cost of incarceration but $35K/year seems about right and perhaps $50K for the legal system and perhaps another $50k in medical and psychological costs, rehab programs, loss of work by their victims etc. According to the BJS non-Hispanic blacks accounted for 39.4% of the prison and jail population in 2009, while non-Hispanic whites were 34.2%, and Hispanics (of any race) 20.6%. According to a 2009 report by the Pew Hispanic Center, in 2007 Latinos "accounted for 40% of all sentenced federal offenders--more than triple their share (13%) of the total U.S. adult population". Again, keep in mind there is not and almost certainly will never be any evidence of a significant genetic difference between Euros and Diverse in psychology, or IQ, and that their greater incidence of problems must be wholly due to their culture.

If one counted only illegals, the crime and imprisonment rate would likely be double that reported for legal Hispanics. As Coulter notes (p101-2) it's impossible to get the actual figures for immigrant crime since it's of course 'racist' to even suggest they should be collected (and as noted, all crime among Diverse is greatly underreported and many Hispanics are misclassified as whites), but it's definitely above that stated, so their actual rate could be near that of blacks. One set of data showed about 1/3 of the 2.2 million state and local prisoners are foreign born and maybe another 5% are American born Hispanics and another 30% black, leaving about 32% white. The foreign born were 70% more likely to have committed a violent crime and twice as likely a class A felony. As Coulter notes, virtually all immigrant groups have a higher crime rate than natives. As the invasion continues, bribery and extortion will see huge increases as they rise to the third world standard. Bribes (the mildest form of extortion) in cash or equivalent is the normal interaction between people in the third world and police, the military, customs and immigration officers, health and fire inspectors, teachers, school admissions officers, and even doctors, surgeons and nurses. I am not guessing here as I spent a decade of my life in the third world and experienced and heard countless stories about all of the above. As time passes, we can expect this to become routine here as well (first of course in California and the Western states) and the nationwide norm thereafter. In addition to continued increases in crime of all kinds we will see the percentage of crimes solved drop to the extremely low levels of the third world. More resources are devoted to the solution of murders than any other crime and about 65% are solved in the USA, but in Mexico less than 2% are solved and as you get further from Mexico City the rate drops to near zero. Also note that the rate here used to be about 80%, but it has dropped in parallel with the increase in

Diverse. Also 65% is the average but if you could get statistics I am sure it would rise with the percent of Euro's in a city and drop as the percent of Diverse increases. In Detroit only 30% are solved. If you keep track of who robs, rapes and murders, it's obvious that black lives matter lots more to Euros than they do to other blacks.

Spanish may become the official and mandatory language and Roman Catholicism the official religion, and of course the Mexican cartels will be the dominant criminal organizations, at least for the Southwestern states by midcentury and likely the whole country by 2100.

Of course, as Coulter points out, it's very hard to get statistics on race and crime or increasingly on race and anything, as its considered 'racism' even to ask and the govt. refuses to collect it. Finding the truth is made much more difficult since Hispanic special interest groups (i.e., third world supremacists), abetted by Euro liberals, who have lost or sold whatever common sense or decency they may have had, are hard at work spreading disinformation with thousands of false or misleading items on the net every week. She does not seem to mention the massive deception facilitated by Yahoo, Bing, Facebook and others, who present among their news items, paid disinformation which presents 'news' that is deliberately false or hugely misleading, such as the item mentioned above (repeated many times a day somewhere on the net) which says that illegals are a good thing as they are paying taxes.

In spite of being given a largely free ride, the Diverse take it all for granted (especially as it's 'racist', 'hate' and 'white supremacist' to point out their free ride, so you won't find it in the major media) and have no problem suing the police, hospitals, and every branch of government for any imagined infraction. The Euros should get a clue and sue them back! They and the US govt, now that Trump is president, could file millions of suits or criminal cases against people who riot in the streets, picket and protest disrupting traffic, smashing windows and causing business losses, psychological trauma, etc. Sue and/or arrest all the criminals and their families for the damages to property, police, loss of business income and work, etc. Also sue the police and every branch of government for failing to protect them every time a crime is committed, especially by illegal Diverse.

As I wrote this the parents of a young San Francisco woman murdered by an illegal alien criminal, who had been deported numerous times, and then shielded from deportation by the San Francisco police (obstruction of justice), is suing them and the feds (and they should sue the board of Supervisors and Governor Brown and the state legislature who voted for the sanctuary rules and Trust Act as well). Predictably he was found not guilty and in the sanctuary city of San Francisco (and now the sanctuary state of California) be able to live out his life of crime while being supported at public expense.

Tens of thousands are robbed, assaulted, raped or murdered by Diverse, and perhaps 100 million victimized in lesser ways every year, and the injured parties (most often Diverse) should sue every time. To facilitate this, the Euros could establish a fund and various organizations to eliminate illegals and crime against Euros. And of course, all the countries that foreign born criminals come from should be forced to pay the cost of policing and prosecuting them and of keeping them here—welfare, medical care, schooling, and their share of all the goods and services mentioned above, including national defense. Mexico should pay all the costs of policing the border and for all the crimes and for all the upkeep of illegals here since day one—i.e., back to say 1965. And they and Colombia should pay for the cost of drug enforcement, addict treatment and jailing, and say a $20 million fine every time someone is raped, disabled or murdered by a drug addict or by an illegal or a naturalized citizen or descendant of a person originating in their country. If they won't we could expel everyone born there and cut off all trade and visas, or just confiscate their oil, mineral and food production. Like many of the ideas here it sounds bizarre because the cowardice and stupidity of 'our' leaders (i.e., not actually ours as we are never asked) has gotten us so used to being abused. We are the last country that should put up with abuse but the politicians and left wing morons have made us the easiest mark on the planet. Yes 9/11 is the most striking abuse, but in fact we suffer as many deaths and injuries from the Diverse every year (e.g., just from drugs and addicts or just from wars), and far more damage every day, if you extrapolate the consequences of their presence here into the future.

Much controversy was generated when Trump mentioned we were letting rapists into the country, but he was just stating the facts. Most crimes in Diverse communities are never reported, often because they are committed by the Hispanic gangs who control them. Coulter recounts a few (the publisher cut the book in half and she says she can easily produce 50 cases for every one cited) of the more outrageous immigrant rape crimes committed here, noting a study in which Latino women here reported childhood sexual abuse at about 80X the rate of other American women, and since it seems likely many did not want to talk about it, it could be higher. She notes that in much of Latin America raping teenagers is not considered a crime (e.g., the age of consent in Mexico is 12) and in any case, it is rare that anything is done about it, since it's often connected to gang members or their families and if you protest you die.

Coulter notes that illegals have made large areas of SouthWestern USA public lands and parks unsafe and some have been closed. Half of some 60 forest fires on federal or tribal land between 2006 and 2010 were started by illegals, many of them set deliberately to avoid capture. The cost of fighting these 30 alone might pay for a good start on a secure border fence.

I assume everyone knows about the massive marijuana growing operations conducted by the Mexican cartels in our national forests. In addition to the erosion and pollution, it is the norm for growers to kill numerous animals and threaten hikers. Most depressing of all is the sellout of the Sierra Club (who suddenly changed their tune after getting a $100 million contribution from billionaire David Gelbaum with the proviso that they support immigration—clearly confused as his right hand protects nature while the left destroys it), who are now devoted to mass immigration, denouncing anyone opposed as "white racists" even when they are Diverse. So, they are another group that should be made to register as an agent of a foreign government and their executives and major contributors made to join the other criminals quarantined on an island (the Aleutians would be perfect but even Cuba would do) where they can't do more harm. Considering the blatant trashing of California by Hispanics, and the clear as day end of nature in America as the immigrants about double the population during the next century or so, this is truly amazing from one viewpoint, but cowardice and stupidity are only to be expected.

One murder in the USA is said to total about $9 million lifetime costs and if they get death it is several million more. At about 15,000/year that would be about $150 billion/year just for homicides-most by Diverse. Mexico has about 5X the murder rate of the USA and Honduras about 20X and your descendants can certainly look forward to our rate moving in that direction. Coulter notes that Hispanics have committed about 23,000 murders here in the last few decades. As I write, this item appeared on the net. "In an undated file photo, Jose Manuel Martinez arrives at the Lawrence County Judicial Building in Moulton, Ala., before pleading guilty to shooting Jose Ruiz in Lawrence County, Ala., in March 2013. Martinez has admitted to killing dozens of people across the United States as an enforcer for drug cartels in Mexico." Not of course rare, just one of the few to make the headlines recently.

Figuring about 2.2 million prisoners (over 1% of the adult population) and a cost to put them in jail from the start of their criminal career of maybe $50,000 each or about $100 billion and the cost to keep them there of about $35,000 each or about $75 billion means a minimum of $150 billion a year, not including other governmental and social costs. I don't see any really clear estimates on the net for the total cost of crime in the USA, but in 2013 it was estimated that violent crime alone cost the UK (where guns are much less frequent and the Mexican and Colombian mafias don't operate significantly) ca. $150 billion or about $6000/household, or about 8% of GDP, but the USA has a much higher percentage of immigrants, guns and drugs, so including all the nonviolent crimes and figuring only 5% of the GDP, that would be about 900 billion per year. Figuring about 60% of crime due to the Diverse, or maybe 80% if you count that of Euros addicted to drugs imported by Diverse, we pay something like 700 billion a year to support Diverse crime.

Of course, all those guilty of felonies, regardless of national origin, history or status could have their citizenship rescinded and be deported or quarantined on an island, where their cost of upkeep could be from $0 to $1000/year rather than $35,000 and it could be made a one-way trip to avoid recidivism. Yes, its sci-fi now, but as the 22nd century approaches and civilization collapses, the tolerance of crime will diminish of necessity. For now, nothing will be done, and crime here will reach the levels in Mexico as the border continues to dissolve and environmental collapse and approaching bankruptcy dissolve the economy. Inside Mexico in 2014 alone, 100 U.S. citizens were known to have been murdered and more than 130 kidnapped and others just disappeared, and if you add other foreigners and Mexicans it runs into the thousands. Even a tiny lightly traveled country like Honduras manages some 10 murders and 2 kidnappings a year of US citizens. And of course, these are the best of times—it is getting steadily worse as unrestrained motherhood and resource depletion bring collapse ever closer.

In another index of how far out of control Mexico is, the criminal cartels, believed to generate well over $21 billion each year from drugs, illegal mining, fishing and logging, theft, prostitution, extortion, kidnapping and embezzlement, are an increasing threat to Pemex, the Mexican oil monopoly. Between 2009 and 2016, thieves tapped the pipelines roughly every 1.4 kms along Pemex's approximately 14,000 km pipeline network, getting more than $1 billion in annual revenue from the gas which they sell on the black market. They are able to do this by terrorizing Pemex employees to obtain info on its operations, offering them the same as they do for everyone in Mexico—silver or lead, i.e., take the bribes or you and your family die.

Euros hear constantly about how bad they are not to want to give the Diverse even more. OK fine, lets agree to do it provided the third world country they are from lets in immigrants until they comprise about 30% of their population, enforces legislation that gives all foreigners in their country, legally or not, citizenship for their babies, welfare, free food, free medical care, free schooling, immunity to deportation, free emergency care, drivers licenses, license to practice law, right to serve on juries, right to bring in all their relatives (who also get all these privileges), right to setup organizations that help them to lie on immigration forms, to evade deportation, to suppress free speech and to subvert the political process so that they can take over the country. Actually, let's make it easy and do it if even one of their countries implements even a few of these. Of course, it will never happen.

Naturally, those with every kind of mental or physical deficiency are dissatisfied with their level of welfare and are getting organized too. Those with autism, actually a spectrum of genetic deficiencies due to as many as 1000 genes, are now campaigning to be regarded as not deficient but 'neurodiverse' and 'neurotypicals' should regard them as peers or even their superiors. No problem for me if someone wants to have a 'friend' or spouse who cannot experience love or friendship and who feels the same when they die as they do when their goldfish does (except being more annoyed by the greater inconvenience). And those with more than mild cases will never hold a job and will be a burden to their relatives and society (i.e., the minority who pay taxes) all their lives, and have a strong tendency to pass the problem on to any offspring they have, so it will likely increase continually, the same as hundreds of other genetic problems with significant heritability. As diagnosis has improved, so has the incidence of autism, which now exceeds 1%, as does that for schizophrenia, schizotypal disorders, ADHD, drug addiction, alcoholism, alexithymia, low IQ, depression, bipolar disorder, etc., etc., so perhaps the combined incidence of disabling mental disorders exceeds 10% and those with physical problems who need partial or complete lifelong support is probably similar, and both are rising in number and percent, the inevitable results of 'civilization', 'democracy' and 'human rights'. Clearly, as the economy collapses, the costs of health care rise, and an ever-larger percentage are nonworking elderly and mentally or physically disabled, this lunatic system will collapse-i.e., the USA will likely have about the same handouts for everyone as third world countries by the early 22nd century—none.

Coulter comments on Mexican citizen Carlos Slim Helu (the world's third richest person as I write this) in the context of the near universal lying about and evasion of immigration issues by the New York Times and other media. He gave a huge loan to the Times a few years ago, to save it from bankruptcy, and this likely accounts for its subsequent failure to cover immigration issues in a meaningful way. Slim is the world's premiere monopolist and his companies control 90% of the Mexican telephone market and many of its major industries (Mexican's refer to their country as Slimlandia). His wealth is the equivalent of roughly 5% of Mexico's GDP. To add perspective, since the USA has about 15 times Mexico's GDP, to be comparable, Bill Gates or Warren Buffet would have to be worth about a trillion dollars each or about 20X their worth. California is the biggest money making US state for Slim, whose take of Mexican goods and services is about $140 million/day. To get the flavor of how things were when Slim managed to acquire the Mexican telephone company (and what can be expected here soon), Gortari (chosen by G.W. Bush to campaign with him) was president of the vicious Mexican political monopoly PRI, and in subsequent years Gortari's brother was found murdered, his relatives were apprehended by Swiss police when they tried to withdraw $84 million from his brother's bank account, and he fled Mexico for Ireland, where he remains. These are among the reasons Coulter calls Slim a robber baron and a baneful influence on Mexico and America. She notes that about $20 billion of Slim's yearly income from his telephone monopoly comes from Mexicans living here. He is Lebanese on both sides, so Mexico has experienced it's own foreign takeover.

The bleeding hearts insist Americans show ever more "humanity" and guarantee our own collapse to help the mob, but what humanity do the Diverse show? They breed like rabbits and consume without restraint, thus condemning everyone, including their own descendants, to Hell on Earth. There is nothing noble about the poor—they are just the rich in waiting. Showing the typical oblivion of the establishment, our Secretary of State Kerry praises China for 'lifting 200 million people out of poverty' but fails to note this placed a huge drain on the world, including their own descendants and that this is unsustainable. Ten or 11 billion (by 2100) all trying to stay out of poverty guarantees the collapse of the world. China's higher QOL, like our own, is only temporary, bought at the cost of their own descendant's and the worlds future.

How much Quality of Life (QOL- a general measure including wealth, crime rate, stress, traffic, drug problems, happiness etc.) might Americans gain by various measures? Banning anchor babies might up QOL 5% by mid-century and 10% by the end relative to doing nothing. Making the ban retroactive to 1982, or preferably to 1898, and thus deporting most of those naturalized by being related to anchor babies, might raise QOL another 5% immediately. Banning immigration might raise it another 10% by end of century, while making the ban retroactive to 1965 and deporting most immigrants along with their descendants and naturalized relatives might give Americans (Diverse and Euros) another 20% more QOL immediately.

And there might be a Back to Africa or Slavery Restitution Act which sent all blacks, or at least those on welfare, unemployed or in prison, back to their homelands so we would never again have to listen to their inane complaints about being kidnapped (as noted, they never consider that if not for slavery they would not exist and if not for colonialism and Euro technology maybe 90% of the people in the third world would not exist), not to mention if not for Euro's they would now be living (or dying) under the Nazi's or the Japanese or the communists. Of course, one could do this on a case by case basis, keeping all the skilled (e.g., medical and high tech personnel). Instead of or prior to the slow deportation process, one could cancel the citizenship or at least the voting privileges of all the naturalized citizens and their descendants since 1965.

The 42 million African-Americans (about 74 million by 2100) who account for 4.5x as many prisoners per capita as Euros, get a largely free ride for all essential services and welfare, take over and render uninhabitable large areas of cities, increase the crowding and traffic by about 13% etc., so they may decrease the QOL of all Americans about 20% on average but to unliveable for those who are in poor neighborhoods. Hispanics amount to about 17% (or about 25% including illegals) and they account for a minimum of 2.5X as many prisoners as Euros and have all the other issues, thus causing a QOL drop of about 30% or again to unliveable in areas they dominate, which soon will include the whole southwestern USA. So overall, it's a fair guess that deporting most Diverse would about double the QOL (or say from bearable to wonderful) right now for the average person, but of course much more increase for the poorer and less for the richer. If one compares likely QOL in 2118 (i.e., a century from now), if all the possible anti-diversity measures were adopted, relative to what it will be if little or nothing is done, I expect QOL would be about 3X higher or again from intolerable to fantastic.

After documenting the incompetence of the INS and the govt., and the countless treasonous and blatantly anti-white racist (in the original meaningful sense of racist) organizations (e.g., the National Council of La Raza) helping to swamp us with immigrants (partial list on p247 of Adios America) Coulter says "The only thing that stands between America and oblivion is a total immigration moratorium" and "The billion dollar immigration industry has turned every single aspect of immigration law into an engine of fraud. The family reunifications are frauds, the "farmworkers" are frauds, the high-tech visas are frauds and the asylum and refugee cases are monumental frauds." Her book is heavily documented (and most data were left out due to size constraints) and of course nearly all the data can be found on the net.

As Coulter notes, a 2015 poll shows that more Americans had a favorable opinion of North Korea (11%) than wanted to increase immigration (7%,) but most Democrats, the Clintons, the Bush's, Obama, casino mogul Sheldon Adelson, Hedge Fund billionaire David Gelbaum, Carlos Slim, Nobel Prize winning economist Paul Krugman and megabillionaire Facebook founder Mark Zuckerberg don't want Americans to ever vote on it. She also mentions that then Florida Governor Jeb Bush (with a Mexican wife) pushed for a bill to give drivers licenses to illegal aliens (copying California) just 3 years after 13 of the 9/11 terrorists had used Florida drivers licenses to board the planes. Yes, the same Jeb Bush who recently called Illegal immigration "an act of love" (of course he means love for Mexico and hatred for the USA, or at least its Euros).

The inexorable collapse of the USA (and other first world countries in Europe are just a step or two behind, as they have let in Diverse who are producing children at about 3 times Euro rates) shows the fatal flaws in representative democracy. If they are to survive and not turn into third world hellholes, they must establish a meritocracy. Change the voting age to 35 minimum and 65 maximum, with minimum IQ 110, proof of mental stability, lack of drug or alcohol dependence, no felony convictions, and a minimum score on the SAT test that would get one into a good college. But the sorry state of what passes for civilization is shown by a recent Gallup poll which found that about 50% of Americans believed the Devil influences daily events, and that UFO's are real, while 36% believe in telepathy and about 25% in ghosts. A yes on any of these would seem to be a good reason for lifetime exclusion from voting and preferably loss of citizenship as should a 'yes' or 'possibly' or 'probably' answer to "Do you think O.J. Simpson is innocent".

Perhaps it will lessen the pain slightly to realize that it is not only the American government that is moronic and treasonous, as versions of its suicide are happening in other democracies. In Britain, the National Children's Bureau has urged daycare teachers to report any 'racist' utterance of children as young as three. About 40% of Britons receive some form of welfare. London has more violent crime than Istanbul or New York and is said to have almost 1/3 of the world's CCTV cameras, which record the average citizen about 300 times a day. Of course, as usual, there are no trustworthy statistics for China, where some of the most successful electronics companies are in the CCTV business and where facial recognition software can often identify any random person in minutes. The UK has the highest rate in Europe of STD's, unwed mothers, drug addiction and abortion. One fifth of all children have no working adult in their house, almost a million people have been on sick leave for over a decade, the courts forced the govt. to give a disabled man money to fly to Amsterdam to have sex with a prostitute because to deny it would be a "violation of his human rights". The number of indictable offenses per 1000 rose from about 10 in the 1950's to about 110 in the 1990's in parallel with the increase in Diverse. Thanks to Mark Steyn's "After America", which is required reading for all bright, civilized Americans who want their country to survive, though barring a military coup, there is not a chance.

Coulter points out the absurdity of politicians fawning on the Hispanic voters (Hispandering). If presidential candidate Mitt Romney had won 71% of the Hispanic vote instead of 27% he still would have lost, but if he had won only 4% more of the white vote he would have won. In fact, 72% of voters are non-Hispanic white, so even if someone got ALL the nonwhite votes, a presidential candidate could still win by a landslide, as we saw in the Trump election. The problem is a sizeable percent of white voters are morons and lunatics who are unable to act in their own self-interest. The absurdity of letting average citizens vote was shown when many were seriously considering Ben Carson for president in 2016--a Seventh Day Adventist bible thumping creationist Detroit ghetto homeboy of such obvious immaturity and stupidity that no sane country would permit him to occupy any public office whatsoever (of course one could say the same of most people and most politicians). He has however, the huge advantage that his defects give him much in common with the average American. It appears to me his limitations include autism-the reason for his famous "flat affect". Do not be fooled by his occasional simulations of laughter--autistics learn to mimic emotions at an early age and some even have successful careers as comedians. Famous comedian Dan Aykroyd had this to say about his Asperger's -- "One of my symptoms included my obsession with ghosts and law enforcement -- I carry around a police badge with me, for example. I became obsessed by Hans Holzer, the greatest ghost hunter ever. That's when the idea of my film Ghostbusters was born."

"Gentle Ben" Carson wants to outlaw abortion, even in cases of rape and incest, thinks we should ditch Medicare, and adheres to many weird conspiracy theories, such as the pyramids not being built by the pharaohs as tombs, but by the biblical Joseph for the storage of grain! He proposes to turn the Department of Education into a fascist overseer of proper morals, with students reporting professors who displayed political bias (i.e., anyone whatsoever) to the government so universities' funding could be cut. "I personally believe that this theory that Darwin came up with was something that was encouraged by the Adversary." The Adversary is a nickname for the devil; it's the actual translation of the word "Satan." He also dismissed the Big Bang, calling it a "fairy tale." Like all creationists, that means that he rejects most of modern science--i.e., everything that lets us make sense of biology, geology, physics and the universe and puts them on all fours with people who lived 100,000 years ago--i.e., Neanderthals. Of course, to the sane, intelligent and educated, "fairy tales" are about heaven, hell, angels and devils, but these are at exactly the right level for the average low class American, Diverse or Euro. Hard to believe we could do worse than Lincoln, Nixon, Reagan, Obama and G.W. Bush, but it will happen, and your descendants will see an endless line of politicians who's only real qualifications are greed, dishonesty, stupidity, dark skin or a Spanish surname. In any case, it's unavoidable in a mobocracy that morons, lunatics and the merely clueless will take over and run the show until it collapses, which is inevitable unless democracy as currently practiced changes radically and Diversity decreases.

Now that we have a reasonably sane, intelligent, patriotic person as president and enough Republicans in congress (the Democrats having sold out their country long ago) we could theoretically deport the illegals, but unless we terminate immigration and retroactively deport most of those naturalized since 1965, it will only slow the disaster and not stop it. However nearly everything Trump tries to do is blocked by the courts and the democrats who long ago ceased to represent America's interests.

Hillary Clinton was preferable to Obama, who was trained as a constitutional lawyer, so he knew our systems fatal weaknesses, and how much further he could go in creating a communist state enforced by fascism, like his much-admired model Cuba. I can easily forgive Hillary for Benghazi and her emails and Bill for Monica, but not for their utterly cynical pardoning of clients of Hillary's brother Hugh, tax cheat Marc Rich and four Hasids convicted in 1999 of bilking the federal government of more than $30 million in federal housing subsidies, small business loans and student grants, in order to curry favor with N.Y. Jews. This is very well known and in fact just about everything I say in this article is easily findable on the net.

Even though our mobocracy is a slow-motion nightmare, if we had a direct democracy (as we easily could in the computer age) and people were actually polled on important issues, perhaps most of our major problems would be disposed of quickly. Suppose tomorrow there was a vote of every registered voter with an email address or smartphone on questions something like this:

Should all illegal aliens be deported within 1year? Should welfare be cut in half within 1year? Should all convicted felons born in another country or one of whose parents were, have their citizenship canceled and be deported within 90 days? Should all immigration be terminated except temporary work visas for those with special skills? Should all child molesters, rapists, murderers, and drug addicts have their citizenship canceled and deported, or if a native citizen, quarantined on an island?

So much the better if voting was restricted to those whose parents and/or all four grandparents are native born, who are non- felons, who have paid more than 5% of their income in taxes the last 3 years and passed mental health, current events and IQ tests. Again, the biggest benefactors would be the Diverse who remained here, but of course the majority will resist any change that requires intelligence or education to grasp.

I am not against a Diverse society, but to save America for your children (recall I have no descendants nor close relatives), it should be capped at say 20% and that would mean about 40% of the Diverse here now would be repatriated. Actually I would not object to keeping the % Diverse we have now (about 37%) provided half the ones here were replaced by carefully screened Asians or by people from anywhere provided they are carefully screened (i.e., no criminals, mental or physical defectives, no religious nuts, no drug addicts, well educated with a proven useful profession), and that they agree to have no more than two children, with immediate deportation if they produce a third, commit a major felony, or remain on welfare for more than one year. And no relatives are permitted entry. In fact, it would be a huge step forward to replace all the Euro criminals, drug addicts, mental cases, welfare users, and chronically unemployed etc. with suitable Diverse. Of course, it's impossible now, but as civilization collapses many amazing things will happen, all of them extremely unpleasant for billions of people, with the Diverse having the most suffering and dying. Coulter jokingly suggests inviting Israel to occupy the border with Mexico, as they have shown how to guard one. However, I would suggest really doing it—either giving them the Southern portion of each border state or perhaps just occupying the border section of Mexico (which we could do in a few days). Israel should be delighted to have a second country, since their position in Israel will become untenable as the USA, France etc. lose the ability to be the world's policemen, and nuclear capable third world countries collapse. However, we should require the Israelis to leave the strict orthodox at home where the muslims will soon get them, as we already have enough rabbit breeding religious lunatics.

Speaking of the collapse of nuclear capable third world countries, it should be obvious that as this happens, possibly before the end of this century, but certainly in the next, with H Bombs in possession of fanatics, it is just a matter of time before they begin vaporizing American and European cities. The only definitive defense will be preemptive "nucleation" of any such country that collapses, or where Muslim radicals take over. It must be obvious to Israel that they will have no other choice but a preemptive strike on Pakistan, Iran and maybe others. Another lovely gift from third world mothers.

In a late 2015 poll by You.Gov, 29 percent of respondents said they can imagine a situation in which they would support the military taking control of the federal government – that translates into over 70 million American adults. And these again are the best of times. At this time in the next century, give or take a few decades, (much sooner in many third world countries), with industrial civilization collapsing, starvation, crime, disease and war worldwide, military coups will be happening everywhere. It's almost certainly the only cure for America's problems, but of course nobody will get to vote on it.

In sum, this is the American chapter of the sad story of the inexorable destruction of the world by unrestrained motherhood. Fifty-one years ago, 396 US politicians voted to embrace the destruction of America by the third world, via the "no significant demographic impact" immigration act. Without the changes they and the Supreme Idiots Court made (along with failure to enforce our immigration laws), we would have about 80 million fewer people now and at least 150 million fewer in 2100, along with tens of trillions of dollars in savings. We would have a chance to deal with the immense problems America and the world face. But, burdened with a fatally fragmented (i.e., Diverse) population about twice the size we might have had, half of which will not contribute to the solution, but rather constitute the problem, it is impossible. What we see is that democracy as practiced here and now guarantees a fatally inept government. Peace and prosperity worldwide will vanish and starvation, disease, crime, military coups, terrorism and warlords will become routine, perhaps in this century, certainly during the next.

To me it's clear that nothing will restrain motherhood and that there is no hope for America or the world regardless of what happens in technology, green living or politics anywhere. Everything tranquil, pure, wild, sane, safe and decent is doomed. There is no problem understanding the stupidity, laziness, dishonesty, self-deception, cowardice, arrogance, greed and insanity of hairless monkeys, but it ought to seem a bit odd that so many reasonably sane and more or less educated people could welcome into their country (or at least permit the entry and tolerate the presence of) large numbers of immigrants who proceed to take over and destroy it. Monkey psychology (shared by all humans) is only capable of seriously considering oneself and immediate relatives for a short time into the future (reciprocal altruism or inclusive fitness), maybe decades at most, so there is no internal restraint. Democracy is the ideal breeding ground for catastrophe.

Most people are neither smart nor well educated, but one can see collapse happening in front of us, and above all in the big urban areas and in the Southwest, especially California and Texas. Sheer laziness, ignorance and a lack of understanding of ecology and the nature of population growth is part of it, but I think that the innate reciprocal altruism we share with all animals must have a big role. When we evolved in Africa we lived in small groups, probably seldom more than a few hundred and often less than 20, and so all those around us were our close relatives, and our behavior was selected to treat them reasonably well as they shared our genes (inclusive fitness) and would reciprocate good deeds (reciprocal altruism). We stopped evolving and began devolving, replacing evolution by natural selection with devolution (genetic degeneration) by unnatural selection about 100,000 years ago, when culture evolved to the point where language, fire and tools gave us a huge advantage over other animals, and there was no longer major selective force for changing behavior or increasing or maintaining health and intelligence. So, to this day we still have the tendency, when we do not feel in immediate physical danger, to act in a more or less friendly manner to those around us. The temporary peace, brought about by advanced communications and weaponry and the merciless rape of the planets resources, has expanded this 'one big family' delusion. Though the more intelligent and reflective persons (which of course includes many Diverse) can see the danger to their descendants, those who are poorly educated, dull witted, or emotionally unstable, sociopathic, autistic, or mentally ill (i.e., the vast majority) won't see it or won't act on it. But how about Adelson, Zuckerberg, Gelbaum, Biden, Clinton, Obama, Krugman and a very long list of the rich and famous? They have at least some education and intelligence, so how can they want to destroy their country and their own children's future? Actually, they are no more well educated, perceptive and future oriented than the average college graduate (i.e., not very), and also, they and their relatives live in gated communities and often have bodyguards, so they will not be seriously concerned about or even aware of trashed neighborhoods, beaches and parks, drive by shootings, home invasions, rapes and murders, nor about paying taxes or making ends meet. They are just not thinking about the fate of their great grandchildren, nor anyone's, or if it does cross their mind, like the vast majority, they don't have clue a about human ecology, nor dysgenics, and can't see the inexorable path to collapse. Insofar as they do, they will not risk personal discomforts by saying or doing anything about it (selfishness and cowardice).

A reader suggested I was talking about 'ethnic cleansing' of Diverse by Euros, but what's happening worldwide is exactly the reverse. I had not actually thought of the destruction of America and industrial civilization by Diverse as genocide, but since the number of Euros of all types (and many groups of Diverse such as Japanese and Koreans) will steadily decline, and their countries be taken over by Diverse, it does have that aspect, though it's the Euros failure to produce enough children that is responsible for their declining numbers. A few zealots (but not so few in the future as Muslims will increase from about 1/5 of the world to about 1/3 by 2100, stimulating the conditions which breed fanaticism) like Al Queda and ISIS want to eliminate all Euro's (and Jews and Sunni's and Feminists and Christians etc., etc.) and the Arabs will certainly demolish Israel by and by, but otherwise there is little motivation to get rid of those who are giving you a free lunch (though of course few Diverse will grasp how big the lunch really is until it stops and civilization collapses). However, as time passes and the competition for space and resources gets ever more desperate, genocide of all Euro groups may become an explicit goal, though mostly it will be far overshadowed by attacks of various Diverse groups on others, which has always been the case and always will. In any event, all Euro and many Diverse groups are certainly doomed--we are talking roughly 2100 and beyond, when the USA (then a part of Mexico) and Europe will no longer have the money or the will to suppress anarchy everywhere, as they will be unable to control it at home.

Shocking as it is for me to come to these realizations (I never really thought about these issues in a serious way until the last 2 years), I don't see any hope for America or the other 'democracies' (America has one foot in Fascism and the other in Communism already) without a drastic change in the way "democracy" works, or in its complete abandonment. Of course, it's going to be pretty much the same elsewhere and both Euros and Diverse ought to pray the Chinese adopt democracy soon (so they collapse too) or they are doomed from outside and inside. That democracy is a fatally flawed system is not news to anyone with a grasp of history or human nature. Our second president John Adams had this to say in 1814:

"I do not say that democracy has been more pernicious on the whole, and in the long run, than monarchy or aristocracy. Democracy has never been and never can be so durable as aristocracy or monarchy; but while it lasts, it is more bloody than either. ... Remember, democracy never lasts long. It soon wastes, exhausts, and murders itself. There never was a democracy yet that did not commit suicide. It is in vain to say that democracy is less vain, less proud, less selfish, less ambitious, or less avaricious than aristocracy or monarchy. It is not true, in fact, and nowhere appears in history. Those passions are the same in all men, under all forms of simple government, and when unchecked, produce the same effects of fraud, violence, and cruelty. When clear prospects are opened before vanity, pride, avarice, or ambition, for their easy gratification, it is hard for the most considerate philosophers and the most conscientious moralists to resist the temptation. Individuals have conquered themselves. Nations and large bodies of men, never." <u>John Adams, The Letters of John and Abigail Adams</u>

The most basic facts, almost never mentioned, are that there are not enough resources in America or the world to lift a significant percentage of the poor out of poverty and keep them there. The attempt to do this is bankrupting America and destroying the world. The earth's capacity to produce food decreases daily, as does our genetic quality. And now, as always, by far the greatest enemy of the poor is other poor and not the rich. Without dramatic and immediate changes, there is no hope for preventing the collapse of America, or any country that follows a democratic system.

So, it is clear that Ann Coulter is right and unless some truly miraculous changes happen very soon, it's goodbye America and hello Third World Hellhole. The only consolations are that we older folk can take comfort in knowing it will not be finalized during our lifetime, that those like myself who are childless will have no descendants to suffer the consequences, and, since the descendants of those who let this happen (i.e., nearly everyone) will be as loathsome as their ancestors, they will richly deserve hell on earth.